the
new
japanese
painting
and
sculpture

An exhibition selected by Dorothy C. Miller and William S. Lieberman

with an essay by William S. Lieberman

The Museum of Modern Art, New York

Distributed by Doubleday & Co., Inc., Garden City, New York

© 1966, The Museum of Modern Art

11 West 53 Street, New York, N. Y. 10019

Library of Congress Catalog Card Number 65-25726

Printed in the U.S.A. by S. D. Scott Printing Co., Inc.

Designed by Joseph Bourke Del Valle

Itinerary

San Francisco Museum of Art, San Francisco, California
April 29-June 13, 1965

Denver Art Museum, Denver, Colorado
October 2-November 14, 1965

Krannert Art Museum, University of Illinois, Urbana, Illinois
December 12, 1965-January 30, 1966

Joslyn Art Museum, Omaha, Nebraska
February 26-March 20, 1966

The Columbus Gallery of Fine Arts, Columbus, Ohio
April 7-May 6, 1966

The Museum of Modern Art, New York
October 17-December 26, 1966

Baltimore Museum of Art, Baltimore, Maryland
January 24-March 19, 1967

Milwaukee Art Center, Milwaukee, Wisconsin
April 13-May 14, 1967

Photographs reproduced in this catalog were generously made available by Hiroshi Akana, Rudolph Burckhardt, Fotografo Clari— AFIP, Geoffrey Clements, Galerie Suzanne De Coninck, Shyu Eguchi, Gutai Pinacotheca, Key Hiraga, Tatsuo Kondo, Shin Kuno, Minami Gallery, Hisayuki Mogami, Sadamasa Motonaga, Ryokichi Mukai, Masanori Obata, Rolf Petersen, Percy Rainford, René Roland, Yoshiyuki Sakai, Kuniharu Sakumoto, Aasa Scherdin, Shimizu, Staempfli Gallery, Soichi Sunami, Mitsuaki Tanaka, Kakuzo Tatehata, Tokyo Gallery, Soichiro Tomioka, Shindo Tsuji, Waichi Tsutaka, United Press International Newspictures, Kazuo Yagi, Takeo Yamaguchi.

Foreword and Acknowledgments

Until very recently, Western awareness of the art of Japan has been restricted to traditional Japanese arts and architecture. In the past few years, however, representations of Japanese art in the biennials in Venice and São Paulo, as well as in the Carnegie and Guggenheim Internationals, have shown some of the remarkable developments in Japanese painting and sculpture which have taken place in the last decade. "The New Japanese Painting and Sculpture" is the largest exhibition of contemporary Japanese art so far presented in the United States. It is a special pleasure for The International Council of The Museum of Modern Art, New York, as part of its program of exchange in the visual arts, to introduce this exhibition to the large audience it will reach while circulating to museums and art galleries in this country. A reciprocal exhibition of recent art from the United States, prepared under the auspices of the International Council, will be seen in Tokyo and Kyoto simultaneously with the present exhibition's New York showing.

The exhibition originated as a project undertaken in collaboration with the San Francisco Museum of Art, where it had its first showing. It was selected by Dorothy C. Miller, Curator of Museum Collections, The Museum of Modern Art, and William S. Lieberman, the Museum's Curator of Drawings and Prints. Selections were made in Japan, Europe, and the United States, and represent forty-six artists, of whom thirty live in Japan, nine in the United States, four in France, and three in Italy. About half the artists are included in a museum exhibition in this country for the first time.

We are grateful to His Excellency Ryuji Takeuchi, Japanese Ambassador to the United States, for generously extending his patronage to the exhibition. Our appreciation also goes to the Kokusai Bunka Shinkokai, Tokyo, and its Managing Director, Kikuji Yonezawa, for assistance in coordinating arrangements in Japan for the exhibition, and to Kusuo Shimizu, Director of the Minami Gallery in Tokyo, who gave invaluable aid in the many details of assembling, framing, and preparing the works in Japan. For their aid in transporting the works, we extend our thanks to the Nippon Yusen Kaisha Line and the Trans-Pacific Freight Conference.

"The New Japanese Painting and Sculpture" was made possible by generous grants from the San Francisco Museum of Art and The JDR 3rd Fund, which supplemented the contribution of the International Council. Thanks are particularly due to Mrs. Walter A. Haas, President of the San Francisco Museum of Art, and George Culler, former Director of the San Francisco Museum, for the support they gave the exhibition, and to Mrs. Bliss Parkinson, President of the International Council when the exhibition originated. We are also especially indebted to Porter McCray, Director of The JDR 3rd Fund, for the advice and encouragement he gave us in preparing the exhibition. Douglas W. Overton, Director

of The Japan Society, New York, generously assisted with preliminary arrangements for the exhibition in both Japan and the United States, for which we express our warmest thanks.

The exhibition was prepared and its itinerary arranged by the Museum's Department of Circulating Exhibitions, under the general supervision of Waldo Rasmussen, Executive Director. George Montgomery assisted in many of the details of research, selection, and assembly. Other members of the Museum staff who aided in preparing the exhibition are: Richard Palmer, who handled the many administrative details; Diana Hallowell, who served both as Registration and Exhibition Assistant; Anne Dahlgren Hecht, Nadia Hermos, Helen M. Franc, and Joan Vass, who worked on the catalog, and Françoise Boas, who supervised its production.

Without the generous cooperation of the artists and lenders, who have parted with their works for two years, the exhibition and its extensive circulation would not have been possible. To these artists and lenders, whose names are listed on page 114, we express our deep gratitude.

Elizabeth A. Straus
President
The International Council of
The Museum of Modern Art, New York

Artists in the Exhibition

Introduction

The long and brilliant development of Japanese art has traditionally been considered to begin in the mid-sixth century, with the introduction of Buddhism from the continent of Asia by way of Korea. Only recently have excavations brought to light from burial mounds and other sites objects such as clay *haniwa,* which exemplify the prehistoric native arts of Japan. These have now joined the Japanese arts of other periods long admired in the West; yet before the twentieth century with its radical revision of taste, the archaic works, had they been known, would undoubtedly—like Cycladic sculpture, pre-Columbian art, and the art of most so-called primitive cultures—have been regarded as of ethnographic rather than artistic interest.

In any event, objects found in the excavations indicate that even before Japan was unified under a single ruler, with a capital in Yamato near Nara, there had already been close connections with the Chinese mainland. With the adoption of Buddhism by the imperial family at the end of the sixth century, foreign influences rapidly increased. From that time until the present, Japanese culture has continually been nourished by outside contacts. Under the stimulus of such foreign influences, Japan has adapted forms and techniques and matured them into separate traditions stamped with her own imprint. Sufficiently removed from their sources, these gradually assimilated influences have become so clearly defined that they must be considered indigenous.

The major conventions of Japanese art were established fourteen hundred years ago, shortly after the introduction of Buddhism. For a thousand years the Korean peninsula, between the Japanese islands and China, continued to serve as a window to the outside world. Portuguese merchants in 1542 were the first Europeans to intrude into Japan; they were soon followed by the Dutch and other Westerners. Religion accompanied commerce, and by 1600 there were more Christians in Japan than there are today. In the arts, previously unfamiliar techniques of painting, methods of draftsmanship, and laws of perspective were swiftly adapted to the Japanese idiom; and these foreign devices are most recognizable when used to depict the foreigners themselves. The direct European influence lasted less than a hundred years. It affected the coastal cities of Kyushu, Japan's southernmost major island, and extended as far as Kyoto on the main island, Honshu, which had been the center for successive courts since the end of the eighth century.

The Tokugawa rule, which consolidated Japan, began in the seventeenth century and lasted about two and a half centuries (from 1615 to 1868). The administrative capital of the government was moved from the somewhat effete Kyoto to the remote village of Edo—present-day Tokyo—northeast of Mount Fuji, whose towering image dominates the Kanto plain and remains a necessary reference for any Japanese.

The Tokugawa era achieved security and peace; it even put an end to the production of firearms, so quickly adopted after having been introduced by the Europeans. Foreigners were first restricted and then expelled. Christianity was suppressed, and international trade discouraged. The degree of insularity enforced by the closed-door policy, however, is often exaggerated. The chief European language was Dutch, and small groups of Japanese eagerly sought and disseminated knowledge from the West, particularly technical information. The crafts of etching and engraving, for instance, had at least one master in Japan at the end of the eighteenth century.

Prosperity and isolation encouraged the arts. The character of creative expression in the Tokugawa era can be attributed to the patronage of the bourgeoisie, rather than to patronage of the court as in preceding periods. The arts which especially flourished were those that appealed to the ascendant merchant class in urban centers. Domestic architecture, crafts, and poetry achieved exquisite perfection; their simplicity, supplanting earlier sumptuousness, belies their extreme sophistication. Kabuki instilled a new realism into drama. Popular fiction and genre painting, less formalized than the other arts, recorded the very earthy pleasures of a "floating world."

Tokugawa culture was confident and self-contained.

When it crystallized, its creative impulse faltered. Tradition became convention, and convention degenerated into repetition, sometimes resulting in such excesses as the enormous and over-elaborate decorations of the temple at Nikko. Significantly, the most successful as well as the most typical examples of the art of the period of seclusion are those conceived on a small scale: objects that can be held in the hand, such as the carved *netsuke* and the glorious creation of Japan's insular retreat, woodblock *ukiyo-e,* the collaborative product of painter, carver, printer, and editor. But by the mid-nineteenth century, even this tradition of printmaking ran dry. Its last great master, the painter Hiroshige, died in 1858, the year in which the United States and Japan signed a "treaty of amity and commerce" and initiated an open-door policy. The coincidence is not unwarranted, for in retrospect, Japanese culture seemed ready to receive fresh stimuli from the outside world.

At first the Japanese were simply curious about the newcomers and their peculiar ways of life. Information about the foreigners was circulated through woodblock prints published in Tokyo. Students of Hiroshige and Kuniyoshi flocked to the new port of Yokohama to record the strangers' appearance, their habits, and their inventions. These painters, with attendant print craftsmen, were the first to popularize Western ideas in a Japanese idiom.

Simultaneously, prints by Japanese artists of previous generations began to be enthusiastically admired abroad by painters and collectors in Europe and, later, the United States. For several decades, in fact, foreign appreciation of Japanese art was restricted to Utamaro, Hokusai, and Hiroshige. Although Western appreciation of Japanese art was based on this limited conception, and in France Japanese prints strongly influenced the post-impressionist painters, particularly Degas, Gauguin, van Gogh, and Toulouse-Lautrec, paradoxically enough it was many years before the Japanese themselves accepted *ukiyo-e* as works of art.

The story of modern Japan begins in 1868, when authority that no divine ruler had possessed for hundreds of years was symbolically restored to the new emperor, Meiji, a boy of sixteen. This restoration of power was idealogically necessary to the emergence of Japan from feudalism into a modern age.

The Emperor Meiji, who ascended the throne in 1867, reigned for forty-five years. His policies were constructive, and the positive force of his personality, as well as his example, furthered the acceptance of Western ideas. Largely because of him, Japan developed as one of the two major powers of Asia, to become in the twentieth century a leader in the modern world.

The impact of foreign technology jolted Japan into a dash toward westernization. The abrupt transition to a modern state was of course reflected in the arts. The results were often chaotic and sometimes lamentable. Lithography (which like the steam engine was introduced into Japan in 1872) together with photography soon obviated the uses of *ukiyo-e.* Lithography's most popular manifestation typifies the ambivalent coexistence of old and new. In 1898 a book dealing with penal reform was issued, containing two styles of illustration: the old system of tortures (abolished in 1873) is described in woodblock, while humane, modern methods (after 1873) are extolled in lithography.

It was inevitable that the industrial revolution, which had occurred so suddenly, should clash with many long-established traditions and conventions, making them seem no longer valid. Western culture was now not merely a curiosity, it was also an ideal. Many Japanese set about to mold themselves after the pattern of foreigners, especially Europeans. Occasionally what they copied was already out of date. To cite a frivolous example, but one nevertheless relevant to the arts, the Emperor Meiji tried to establish the ambience of a court with the colors and manners of Napoleon III's. Although by no stretch of the imagination could his court be considered the equivalent of anything in Europe, its leisures and pleasures included such innovations as the waltz, horse racing, the piano, and the bustle.

This attempt to create a sophisticated elite was not successful. No common meeting ground was established between artists and those privileged by birth or money; nor was there, as in the Tokugawa era, an informed and cultivated bourgeoisie committed to the new regime, who together with an intelligentsia might have given significant encouragement and appreciation to the arts. Even today, the relation between creators and patrons of the arts has not been resolved in Japan.

In 1871, the Ministry of Education published a serious study of Western art. During the next two decades, private schools for Western techniques of painting and drawing became fashionable. In 1889, a group of professional artists banded together as an exhibiting society for painters in oil; and at the turn of the century a popular novel, analogous to Murger's earlier *Scènes de la Vie de Bohème,* romanticized the life of the art student in Paris. A thorough treatise on impressionism was printed in 1915. Artists imported from Italy introduced academic painting, sculpture, and architecture.

The most important event in the development of Western art in Japan took place in 1912, the year of the Emperor Meiji's death. A large exhibition of Rodin's sculpture and drawings was organized in Tokyo. For a few Japanese artists, it had an impact which to a certain extent may be compared to the wider effect that the Armory Show, held in New York, Boston, and Chicago the following year, had upon American artists. The response of the general public in Japan to the Rodin exhibition, however—unlike that of the American public to the Armory Show—was negligible.

During the late years of Meiji's reign and that of his son, Japan produced some excellent artists whose work is better than competent and deserves an international audience. These artists painted in oil on canvas—or, as the Japanese still insist, in "Western style." They studied in France, Italy, and sometimes Germany, and on their return home became influential and to a certain extent revered. Their paintings are unknown abroad and in Japan today are too often dismissed by those most concerned with contemporary art. On the other hand, as a result of recent foreign interest, the applied arts of the Meiji era are now much sought after by the Japanese.

Literature met the challenge of westernization sooner and more successfully than the visual arts. In painting, the female figure portrayed in the nude offended the sensibilities of many Japanese, and

8

unorthodox theories threatened those who worked in traditional styles. Most serious was the fact that the Japanese tended too quickly to deny their indigenous culture. The American scholar Ernest Fenollosa was among the first to express concern. From his arrival in Japan in 1878 until his death in 1908, he, more than any Japanese, was responsible for preserving the nation's pride in its unique heritage in the arts. A reaction against the onslaught of modernization was both necessary and inevitable.

Politically, three insurrections were suppressed between 1876 and 1884. The Boxer Rebellion in China, Japan's victory over Russia in 1905, and the First World War soon after thrust Japan well into the twentieth century. By 1926, Japan had achieved an outward resemblance to those foreign peers in Europe she had chosen to emulate. The transformation was remarkable but superficial. To a European or American, the success of Japanese modernization was demonstrated by the country's growing economy and efficient, apparently stable, government, rather than by the arts—which still remained exotic to foreign eyes. Actually, the transformation had been too rapid. The revolution had been peaceful, but it had been precipitous. Japan was a country in which tradition, a ritual of discipline rather than of belief, attended every detail of public and private life. Although modernization had been accomplished without foreign domination, it was without internal roots. There was no precedent for the direction of the future, and the right path was not found.

Throughout the 1930s, Japan's burning ambition to achieve equality with major world powers and her need to secure the natural resources vital to her industrial development led her to adopt an increasingly militant policy. This culminated in her invasion of the Asian mainland and ultimate involvement in the Second World War. Catastrophic defeat left Japan in a state of collapse and destroyed a system of life and government which the Japanese for centuries had been taught to hold sacred. For the first time in her civilized history, Japan submitted to foreign rule. The occupation indoctrinated a new generation with values and desires which, for better or worse, could in no way be reconciled with conventional precepts of the past. The demarcation between generations and their attitudes thus became sharply defined.

Once again, Japan set about adapting herself to the outside world. Although this time the United States, rather than Europe, served as a model, in respect to the arts Japan's outlook was international.

A discussion of modern Japanese art must be prefaced by many general observations that may be worth enumerating here. First, one hundred years has been a short time in which to absorb the complete heritage of Western civilization. Second, the casual visitor to Tokyo may be tempted to recognize equivalents to what he may expect in the artistic ambience of London, New York, Paris, or Rome; but such similarities are superficial and have no resemblance in fact or practice to European or American counterparts. Third, anything that can be transmitted by print, any word or photograph, quickly finds its way to Japan, where it is read and reproduced. Fourth, fiction, film making, and architecture are the most vital arts of Japan today. Fifth, sculpture has not been as swift as painting to realize Western goals. Sixth, in painting, the assumption that Western methods and models are desirable, and therefore the best and most progressive, has encouraged novelty but created confusion. Seventh, too many specialists act zealously and often jealously as entrepreneurs of contemporary Japanese culture, particularly in the visual arts. Last, and incredibly, the quantity of paintings produced in Japan exceeds that of any other country in the world.

The fantastic amount of activity in the arts in Tokyo simulates that in any international art capital. Exhibitions occur with bewildering frequency in department stores, museums, municipal halls, and hundreds of small commercial galleries. Lavishly produced catalogs and books and splendidly illustrated magazines are available everywhere. Newspapers subsidize, indeed organize, exhibitions and whenever possible agitate their readers into a frenzy of attendance. Although these exhibitions are well attended, and although industries, banks, business firms, and hotels commission or acquire significant works, there are still no more than a dozen private collectors of modern art in Japan, and of these only a few collect works by modern Japanese artists.

There is in fact little place in a Japanese home for collectors to display what they acquire. A typical Japanese room reserves one small area, sometimes recessed, for a single work of art—usually a *kakemono* (wall hanging). Since 1900, a well-to-do bourgeois house has had as an appendage one Western-style room with chairs, antimacassars, raised tables, and solid walls. Such areas, however, are demonstrable symbols of affluence and see little use in everyday life. The few extensive collectors of modern paintings are among the very rich. They amass works of art in storehouses adjacent to their dwellings or find satisfaction in creating their own museums.

Tokyo and, more recently, Kyoto have national museums of modern art. Their collections, devoted exclusively to the works of Japanese artists, are not continuously on view. Group exhibitions of Japanese artists are selected by committees which rely heavily upon nominations by government officials and art critics. The organization of international exhibitions, frequently retrospectives of foreign artists, is generally assumed by newspapers.

A third national institution, The Museum of Western Art in Tokyo, was conceived by the French government after the Second World War. Its activities in modern art remain dominated by the School of Paris. In Kamakura, the municipal Museum of Modern Art (international) unfortunately lacks adequate civic support. The best over-all representations of Western art belong to private museums, the Ishibashi (Bridgestone) Gallery in Tokyo and the Ohara Museum in Kurashiki. The direction of both museums is enlightened, and their collections are extraordinary. In Nagaoka, in the northern prefecture of Niigata, the modest Museum of Contemporary Art, privately supported, specializes in collecting and exhibiting recent trends in Japanese, as well as American and European, painting and sculpture. It is the only museum in Japan that is a lender to this exhibition.

Art dealers concerned with Western art (in the Japanese sense of "modern painting in oil") are privileged to display proudly and prominently as a trademark a palette cast in metal. The three galleries in Japan that are lenders to this exhibition constitute a source of practical encouragement and appreciation for

9

the artists they represent. Unfortunately, they are exceptional; the average dealer merely sells facilities for one-shot exhibitions, which may last only six or seven days. He makes no effort to represent an individual artist nor to further his career.

Since Japanese artists have so little encouragement from other sources, their numerous societies provide a very necessary moral support. Artists' associations proliferate, divide, and split. To name a very few among hundreds (several of which are referred to in the biographical notes in this catalog), there are the Activist Society, the Art Culture Society, the Free Art Society, the Free Artists Society, the Gutai Association, the Ichiyo Society, the Issui Society, the Independent Art Center, the Independent Artists Society, the Japan Academy of Art, the Japanese Artist Association, the Modern Art Association, the National Painting Society, the New Tree Society, the New Works Society, the Nika Association and the Niki Association (both of which are powerful, and both of which have had two incarnations); and of shorter but more lively duration, the Kyoto Five, the Young Seven (Tokyo), the Anti-Independent Group, the New Stream of Kyushu, and simply, the Sweet.

These associations differ in their organization and importance. Some have elaborate programs, a few are protest groups, several exist for only one or two seasons. Several societies which began as avant-garde are today reactionary victims of their own academies. Membership varies: some societies are highly exclusive and may consist of only three or four individuals, while others may embrace hundreds. Since group loyalties are intense, it is often difficult to meet any artist without encountering the entire membership of his particular group. Intergroup rivalries are equally intense, particularly among the older generation.

The specific function of the artists' societies is the preparation of annual exhibitions of their members' work, which are usually displayed in vast municipal halls in Tokyo, Nagoya, Kyoto, and Osaka, as well as in provincial cities removed from the Tokaido Road. Informal groups with small membership may rent commercial galleries, usually in Tokyo. These showings may be an artist's only chance to present one or two paintings to the public.

Unless a painter or sculptor belongs to an association, has independent means, or captures a voluble critic who can propagandize his work, he has no opportunity to exhibit. One-man shows of living native artists are seldom retrospective and are never organized by national museums. Artists fortunate enough to obtain or arrange scheduled exhibitions at commercial galleries paint specifically for those occasions. Even for international art exhibitions such as the biennials in Venice and São Paulo (in which each nation generally represents the artists selected by several works), the Japanese participants are usually chosen by committees sufficiently far in advance to allow the production of a body of work especially intended for international competition. The swiftest road to success at home unfortunately remains acceptance abroad.

The difficulties that afflict the artist in most countries today—the inability to earn a livelihood through painting or sculpture alone, and the necessity of supplementing his earnings by teaching at a university or acting as an art director for an industry or publication—are perhaps even more acute in Japan than elsewhere. In addition, since Japan is one of the most crowded countries in the world, space in which to paint or sculpt remains a constant problem.

Fellowships and awards, largely from foreign foundations, make it possible for Japanese artists to travel abroad but until recently have seldom been given to the avant-garde or to the young. Too frequently, an artist's exposure to a mass of foreign impressions comes so late in his development that the experience is no more than unsettling.

The vast majority of painters in Japan work in a realistic idiom, in either traditional or Western styles. Schools and universities teach both methods, and students, like their teachers, specialize in one or the other. The conventions of traditional painting on paper with stone pigments derive from the Chinese, and to Western eyes often resemble drawing. (Conversely, Japanese painters of abstractions in Western style are seldom draftsmen.)

The best representational painting, without doubt, appears in traditional styles and media. Its most characteristic examples are those least contaminated by Western influence. These paintings illustrate a mode of expression tuned by centuries of practice; they combine direct observation of nature, decorative balance of design, and suggestive economy of detail. The paper itself furnishes elements of space and color. A selection of contemporary work thus characterized by technique and identified with tradition should in fact be organized for an international audience.

Naturalistic "Western-style" painting attracts many Japanese who regard its technique and exactitude as a standard to be emulated. Several figurative artists who paint in oil on canvas command tremendous prices. The best of these painters are over fifty. They combine heavy impasto with expressionistic distortion, and their choice of theme often assumes an authentic universality. Too often, however, such paintings are saturated with sentiment that romantically evokes the stereotypes most foreigners hold of an exotic Japan: the geisha forever powdered white, the heroes of Noh and Kabuki, the samisen player in repose, the strutting samurai. Paintings of classical monuments and such architectural details as tiled roofs similarly glorify the past. In landscapes, extremes of weather are understandably frequent, while the image of Fuji is so dominant that even other mountains seem painted to resemble it.

Human figures, animals, city scenes, landscapes, and still lifes are perhaps treated more originally by certain printmakers who, shortly after the war, merged Western techniques of woodcut with a bold and decorative, and older, tradition of Japanese printmaking. Modern woodcuts were the first examples of contemporary Japanese art to be seen abroad after the Second World War. They were collected by foreigners, popularized by American literati, and therefore publicized at home. The vigor and vitality of these woodcuts seemed about to burgeon; but today their production, except by three or four artists, is directed at the tourist trade.

Between the two wars, many artists evolved styles based on earlier fauve and German-expressionist prototypes; during the 1930s, photographic surrealism was much admired. After the war, the Japanese developed a violent attraction to abstract, non-representational art. Today, painters of abstract compositions in oil are the best and most original artists of Japan; several are included in this exhibition.

The forty-six artists in the present exhibition were chosen in 1964. Intended for an American audience, the selection reflects a choice that probably would not have been made at that time by the Japanese themselves and includes many artists now resident abroad. Calligraphy and traditional-style painting on paper are not represented, nor is any work by printmakers—who until recently were considered painters by the Japanese. The exhibition is concerned only with Japanese art of international tendency. Most of the works included were executed between 1960 and 1965, although three artists are represented by earlier paintings and sculpture. To suggest the course of development more clearly, the arrangement in this catalog (except in the color plates and checklist) is by chronological order according to the artists' birth dates.

Although the exhibition is in no way a definitive survey of modern art in Japan, it nevertheless indicates some directions that seem especially vital today. The Museum of Modern Art feels privileged to present the exhibition to the American public, in the hope that it may focus attention not only on these particular artists and their work, but on the entire course of development now taking place among Japanese-born artists. If one may predict the future from the past, few can doubt that in the twentieth century, as so often before in her history, Japan will benefit by international contacts and stimuli from abroad, and from her native genius will produce an art distinctively her own.

William S. Lieberman

Domoto: *Solution of Continuity, 57.* 1963. 12-part screen, aluminum and canvas, each panel 63$\frac{1}{8}$ x 15$\frac{3}{4}$". Lent by the artist.

Motonaga: *Untitled.* 1963. Oil and gravel on canvas, 72⅛ x 50¼".
Tokyo Gallery, Tokyo.

Above, Saito: *Untitled (red)*. 1962. Oil on wood, 71³/₄ x 47³/₄".
Mrs. John D. Rockefeller 3rd, New York.

Tsutaka: *Untitled*. 1964. Oil on canvas, 46 x 31³/₄".
Yamada Art Gallery, Kyoto.

Above, Inokuma: *Wall Street.* 1964. Oil on canvas, 80⅛ x 70⅛″.
San Francisco Museum of Art. Gift of Mrs.
Madeleine Haas Russell.

Right, Onosato: *Untitled.* 1962. Oil on canvas, 28⅞ x 36″.
Mr. and Mrs. John D. Rockefeller 3rd, New York.

16

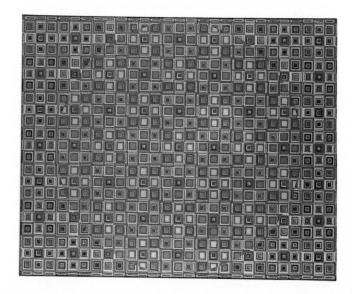

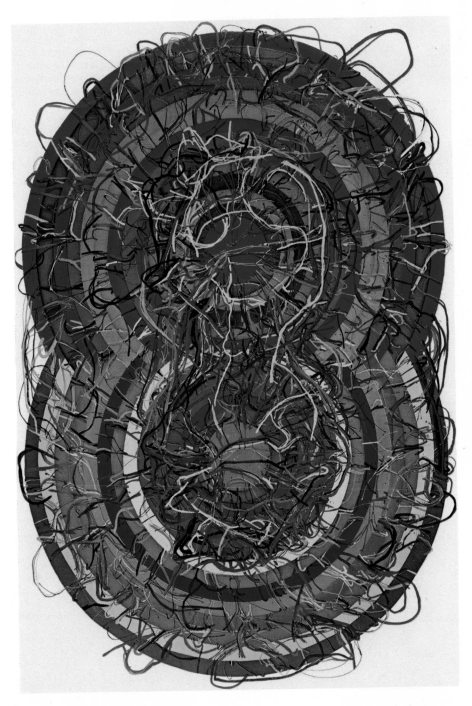

Tanaka: *Untitled*. 1964. Vinyl on canvas, 88⅞ x 131⅜".
The Museum of Modern Art, New York. Purchase.

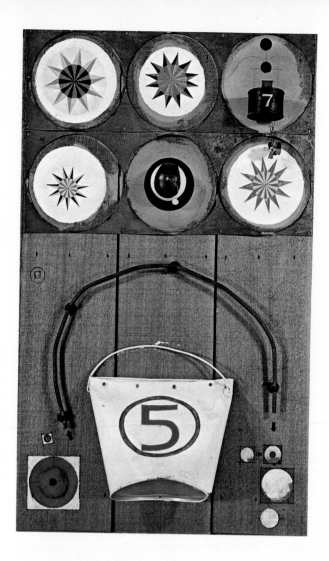

Left top, Kikuhata: *Roulette: Number Five*. 1964. Enamel paint and assemblage on wood, 42 1/8 x 25 1/2 x 8 1/2". The Museum of Modern Art, New York. Purchase.

Left bottom, Nakanishi: *Compact Objects (6)*. 1962. Assemblages contained in polyester, each 9 x 5 7/8 x 5 7/8". Lent by the artist; Mrs. John D. Rockefeller 3rd, New York; Mrs. Warren Tremaine, Santa Barbara, California; and The Museum of Modern Art, New York (Purchase).

Below, Okamoto: *A Western Dog*. 1964. Acrylic on canvas, 35 1/4 x 51 1/4". George Montgomery, New York.

Right, Kojima: *Untitled (Figure)*. 1964. Painted plaster, cloth and polyester, 68 5/8 x 43 3/4 x 18 1/4". Lent anonymously.

Left, Kawabata: *Dark Oval.* 1964. Oil on canvas, 63⅞ x 51⅜".
Mrs. John D. Rockefeller 3rd, New York.

Kawashima: *Untitled 1964, New York.* 1964. Oil on canvas,
100½ x 80". The Museum of Modern Art, New York. Purchase.

20

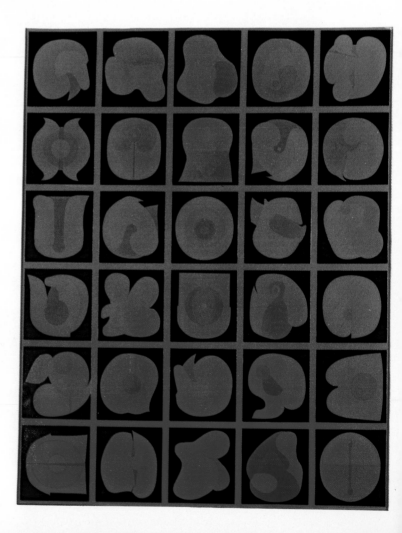

The Artists and their Work

Takeo Yamaguchi

Born in Seoul, Korea, 1902. Graduated from Tokyo University
of Arts, 1927. Studied under Eisaku Wada; in France, under
Yuzo Saeki and Ossip Zadkine, 1927-1930. Member of Nika
Association, Tokyo, since 1931; exhibited with them. Lives in
Tokyo; teaches at Musashino Art School. *One-man shows:*
Minami Gallery, Tokyo, 1961; Nihonbashi Gallery, New York,
1963. In various group exhibitions, including III and VII Bienal,
São Paulo, 1955, 1963; XXVIII Biennale, Venice, 1956;
Guggenheim International Award Exhibition, New York, 1958;
"Six Japanese Painters," Gres Gallery, Washington, D. C., 1960.
Awarded prize at Contemporary Japanese Art Exhibition,
Tokyo, 1954; one by Japanese Minister of Culture,
1962. Represented in collections of Brooklyn Museum,
Brooklyn, N.Y.; Municipal Museum, Kagoshima; Museum of
Modern Art, Kamakura; Ishibashi Cultural Center, Kurume;
Solomon R. Guggenheim Museum, New York; Museum of
Modern Art, New York; Museu de Arte Moderna, São Paulo;
National Museum of Modern Art, Tokyo.

T. Yamaguchi: *Enshin.* 1961. Oil on wood, 71$\frac{7}{8}$ x 71$\frac{7}{8}$". Minami Gallery, Tokyo.

Genichiro Inokuma

Born in Takamatsu City, Kagawa Prefecture, 1902. Studied at Tokyo Academy of Fine Arts, 1922-1926. Founder of Shinseisaku Association, Tokyo, 1936. Taught painting, Tokyo Academy, 1937-1940. Visited Europe, 1940. Conducted his own art school in Japan, 1945-1955. To U.S.A., 1955; lives in New York. *One-man shows:* Willard Gallery, New York, 1956, 1957, 1958, 1960, 1962, 1964. In various group shows since 1927, including Salon des Indépendants, Paris, 1938; I and V Bienal, São Paulo, 1951, 1959; Salon de Mai, Paris, 1952; Carnegie International Exhibition, Pittsburgh, 1952, 1958, 1961, 1964; "Contemporary Japanese Painting and Sculpture," circulated by American Federation of Arts, 1963-64. Awarded Mainichi Cultural and Artistic Prize for mural paintings, 1952; a first prize, Japanese Contemporary Artists Exhibition, Tokyo, 1964. Commissioned to do murals for Keio University, Tokyo, 1947; Maruei Hotel, Nagoya, 1952; Tokyo Central Station, 1953; Takashimaya Department Store, New York, 1958; Municipal Building of Kagawa Prefecture, Japan, 1959. Represented in collections of Baltimore Museum of Art, Baltimore; Institute of Contemporary Arts, Boston; San Francisco Museum of Art; National Museum of Modern Art, Tokyo; and others.

Inokuma: *Wall Street.* 1964. Oil on canvas, 80⅛ x 70⅛". San Francisco Museum of Art. Gift of Mrs. Madeleine Haas Russell.

Yoshishige Saito

Born in Tokyo, 1904. Graduated from Nihon High School, Tokyo, 1924. Studied at Surugadai Art Studio, Tokyo. A founder of Modern Art Association, Tokyo, 1939; member until 1953. Traveled to Europe, 1960. Has taught at Tama College of Fine Arts, Tokyo, since 1964. Lives in Yokohama City, Kanagawa Prefecture. *One-man shows:* Tokyo Gallery, Tokyo, 1958, 1960 (2), 1962, 1963; Galleria Naviglio, Milan, 1964; Galerie Friedrich-Dahlem, Munich, 1964; Kunstverein, Freiburg, 1965. In many group shows since 1933, including Carnegie International Exhibition, Pittsburgh, 1956; V and VI Bienal, São Paulo, 1959, 1961; XI Premio Lissone, Lissone (Italy), 1959; Guggenheim International Award Exhibition, New York, 1960; XXX and XXXII Biennale, Venice, 1960, 1964; "Japanische Malerei der Gegenwart," Akademie der Künste, Berlin, 1961. Awarded prizes at International Art Exhibition, Tokyo, 1957, 1959; Contemporary Art Exhibition, Tokyo, 1958, 1960; V and VI Bienal, São Paulo, 1959, 1961; Guggenheim International Award Exhibition, 1960. Commissioned to do mural by Museum of Contemporary Art, Nagaoka. Represented in collections of Museum of Modern Art, Kamakura; National Museum of Modern Art, Kyoto; Museum of Contemporary Art, Nagaoka; National Museum of Modern Art, Tokyo.

Saito: *Untitled (red).* 1962. Oil on wood, 71³/₄ x 47³/₄".
Mrs. John D. Rockefeller 3rd, New York.

Saito: *Untitled (blue).* 1962. Oil on wood, 71⅝ x 47¾". Howard E. Johnson, Oakland, California.

Jiro Yoshihara

Born in Osaka City, Osaka Prefecture, 1905. Graduated from Commercial School of Kwansei Gakuin University, Nishinomiya. 1954, founded Gutai Art Association, Osaka; active in it since. Traveled in U.S.A. and Europe, 1958, 1965. Lives in Ashiya City, Hyogo Prefecture. *One-man shows:* Asahi Kaikan Hall, Osaka, 1928; Kinokuniya Art Gallery, Tokyo, 1937. In many group shows since 1934, including Salon de Mai, Paris, 1952; Carnegie International Exhibition, Pittsburgh, 1952, 1958, 1961; XII Premio Lissone, Lissone (Italy), 1961; "Japanische Malerei der Gegenwart," Akademie der Künste, Berlin, 1961; "Contemporary Japanese Painting and Sculpture," circulated by American Federation of Arts, 1963-64; "Contemporary Japanese Painting," Corcoran Gallery of Art, Washington, D.C., 1964; Guggenheim International Award Exhibition, New York, 1964. Won prizes at Nika Exhibitions, Tokyo, 1937, 1939, 1949; Osaka Prefectural Art Award, 1953; Hyogo Prefectural Cultural Award, 1963. Commissioned to do drop curtains for Asahi Kaikan Hall, Osaka, 1950, and Isen Kaiken Hall, Okayama, 1953; art work for various stage productions; mural for lobby of Nishi Chobori Housing Area. Represented in collections of Museum of St. Louis University, St. Louis, Mo.; Carnegie Institute, Pittsburgh; International Center of Aesthetic Research, Turin.

Yoshihara: *Untitled.* 1962. Oil on canvas, 71⅝ x 107¼". Michel Tapié, Paris.

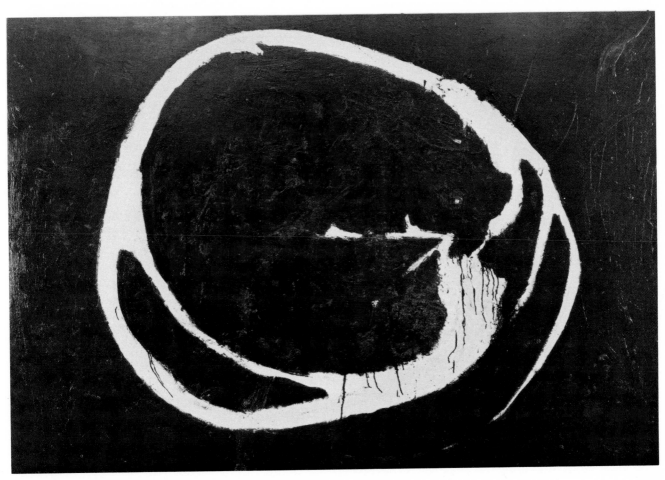

Key Sato

Born in Oita City, Oita Prefecture, 1906. Graduated from
Tokyo Academy of Fine Arts, 1929. Studied under Takeji
Fujishima and, 1930-1934, at Académie Colarossi, Paris.
Returned to Japan, 1934. A founder of Shinseisaku Association,
Tokyo. 1952, returned to Paris, where he now lives. *One-man
shows:* Sanmaido Gallery, Tokyo, 1934; Tokyo Gallery, Tokyo,
1951, 1954; Galerie Mirador, Paris, 1954; Galerie Jacques
Massol, Paris, 1959, 1960, 1961, 1964; Hamilton Galleries,
London, 1964; World House Galleries, New York, 1965. In many
group shows since 1926, including Salon d'Automne, Paris,
1931-1933; Carnegie International Exhibition, Pittsburgh, 1952,
1964; Salon de Mai, Paris, 1956-1959; XXX Biennale, Venice,
1960. Represented in collections of Atheneum Art Collection,
Helsinki; Museum of Modern Art, Kamakura; Tate Gallery,
London; Musée National d'Art Moderne, Paris; Musée
Communal, Verviers, Belgium.

Sato: *Of the Essence.* 1960-63. Oil on burlap, 36⅛ x 28⅝".
Lent by the artist.

30

Sato: *History of Space (black)*. 1965. Oil on canvas, 63⅞ x 51¼″. Mrs. John D. Rockefeller 3rd, New York.　　31

Shindo Tsuji

Born in Tottori City, Tottori Prefecture, 1910. Studied painting at Yodobashi Independent Art Study Center, 1932-1933; sculpture at Taninaka Japan Art Institute Study Center, 1935-1939. Taught at Kyoto Junior Art College, 1939; since 1950, at Kyoto Municipal College of Fine Arts, where he is now a full professor. Visited Europe, 1963. Lives in Kyoto. *One-man shows:* Maruzen Gallery, Tokyo, 1952, 1954, 1956; Nihonbashi Gallery, Tokyo, 1961; Beni Gallery, Kyoto, 1964. In many group exhibitions since 1953, including IV Bienal, São Paulo, 1957; "Seven Sculptors," Solomon R. Guggenheim Museum, New York, 1958; XXIX Biennale, Venice, 1958; Carnegie International Exhibition, Pittsburgh, 1961; "Contemporary Japanese Painting and Sculpture," circulated by American Federation of Arts, 1963-64. Commissioned works include sculpture for roof, Osaki Kabuki Theater, 1958; mural, Yokohama City Hall, 1959; relief design and mural, Nisei Theater, Tokyo, 1963; sculpture, Namerikawa City Hall, 1963. Represented in collections of Museum of Modern Art, Kamakura; Carnegie Institute, Pittsburgh; Library, Tokyo University of Arts.

Left, Tsuji: *Jomon.* 1959. Terra-cotta, 45¼ x 17⅝ x 7½″. Yamada Art Gallery, Kyoto.

Right, Tsuji: *Han Shan.* 1961. Terra-cotta, 39 x 24¾ x 9″. Mr. and Mrs. John D. Rockefeller 3rd, New York.

32

Waichi Tsutaka

Born in Nishinomiya City, Hyogo Prefecture, 1911. Studied at
Nakanoshima Western Art Center, Osaka, 1942-1944.
Traveled in Canada, U.S.A. (West Coast), Central and South
America 1959-1960; Italy, Switzerland, France and
England, 1962-1963. Lives in Nishinomiya. *One-man shows:*
Fujikawa Gallery, Osaka, 1950; Formes Gallery, Tokyo, 1950;
Umeda Gallery, Osaka, 1954, 1955; Minami Gallery, Tokyo,
1959, 1960; Galeria Tenreiro, São Paulo, 1959, 1960; Hitsuguya
Gallery, Hiroshima, 1963; Motomachi Gallery, Kobe, 1963;
Shimanouchi Gallery, Osaka, 1963; Saigado Gallery,
Hamamatsu City, 1965; others in Japan, South America and
Italy. In many group exhibitions since 1947, including "Six
Contemporary Japanese Artists," Smithsonian Institution,
Washington, D. C., 1956; IV and V Bienal, São Paulo, 1957, 1959;
Guggenheim International Award Exhibition, New York, 1960;
"Japanische Malerei der Gegenwart," Akademie der Künste,
Berlin, 1961; "Contemporary Japanese Abstract Art,"
National Museum of Modern Art, Tokyo, 1963. Awarded prize,
Contemporary Japanese Art Exhibition, Tokyo, 1958.
Commissioned works include mural, Nishinomiya Health Center,
Hyogo Prefecture, 1955; mural, Kansai Theater, Kobe, 1956;
mural, Kobe Branch Building, Kansai Electric Power Company,
1964; wall relief, Shiobara Institute High School, Kobe, 1965.
Represented in collection of Museu de Arte Moderna, São Paulo.

Tsutaka: *Cosmos*. 1963. Oil on canvas, 35³/₄ x 25⅞".
Lent by the artist.

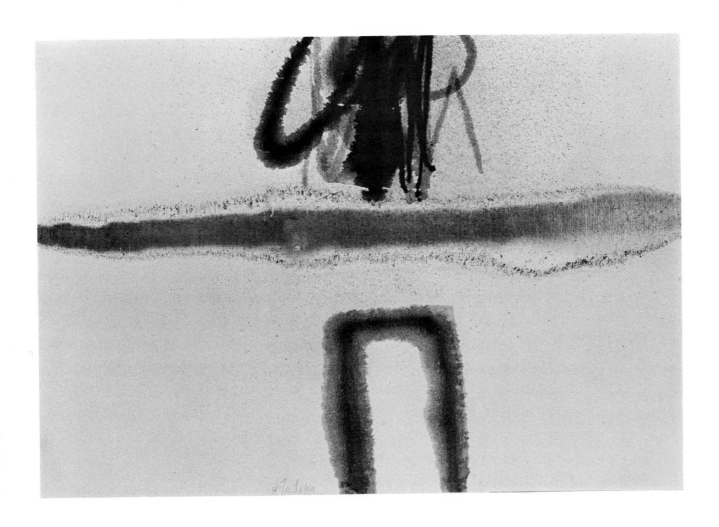

Tsutaka: *Accept the Inevitable.* 1964. Oil on canvas, 51¼ x 76″. Mrs. Donald B. Straus, New York.

Minoru Kawabata

Born in Tokyo, 1911. Graduated from Tokyo Academy of Fine
Arts, 1934. Studied art in Paris and Italy, 1937-1939. Professor
of art, Tama College of Fine Arts, Tokyo, 1950-1955. Taught
at New School for Social Research, New York, 1958-1961.
Returned to Japan, 1963-1964. Lives in New York. *One-man
shows:* Mitsukoshi Gallery, Tokyo, 1940; Matsuya Gallery,
Tokyo, 1958; Betty Parsons Gallery, New York, 1960, 1961,
1963, 1965; Galleria Apollinaire, Milan, 1961. In various group
exhibitions, including I, IV and V Bienal, São Paulo, 1951, 1957,
1959; Salon de Mai, Paris, 1952; Carnegie International
Exhibition, Pittsburgh, 1958, 1961; Guggenheim International
Award Exhibition, New York, 1958, 1964; XXXI Biennale, Venice,
1962. Awarded Saburi Prize, Tokyo, 1940; Kamakura Prize,
Tokyo, 1958; Guggenheim International Award, New York,
1958; a prize at São Paulo Bienal, 1959. Represented in
collections of Museu de Arte Moderna, São Paulo; National
Museum, Tokyo; National Museum of Modern Art, Tokyo.

Kawabata: *Dark Oval.* 1964.
Oil on canvas, 63⁷/₈ x 51³/₈".
Mrs. John D. Rockefeller 3rd,
New York.

Kawabata: *March*. 1964. Oil on canvas, 63³/₄ x 51³/₈″. Betty Parsons Gallery, New York.

Toshinobu Onosato

Born in Iida City, Nagano Prefecture, 1912. Studied painting in Seifu Tsuda studio, 1931-1934. Exhibited with Nika Association, Tokyo, 1935; member of Jiyu Art Association, Tokyo, 1938-1956. In Manchuria, 1941-1945. Prisoner-of-war, Siberia, 1945-1948. Traveled in Europe and U.S.A., 1964. Has lived in Kiryu City, Gumma Prefecture, since 1922. *One-man shows:* Takemiya Gallery, Tokyo, 1953; Mimatsu Gallery, Tokyo, 1955; Kabutoya Gallery, Tokyo, 1958; Gres Gallery, Washington, D.C., 1961; Minami Gallery, Tokyo, 1962. In various group exhibitions since 1954, including "Contemporary Trend of Japanese Paintings and Sculptures," National Museum of Modern Art, Kyoto, 1964; Guggenheim International Award Exhibition, New York, 1964; XXXII Biennale, Venice, 1964; "Moderne Malerei aus Japan," Kunsthaus, Zurich, 1965. Awarded Grand Prize, VII Biennial, Tokyo, 1963. Represented in collections of Museum of Contemporary Art, Nagaoka; National Museum of Modern Art, Tokyo.

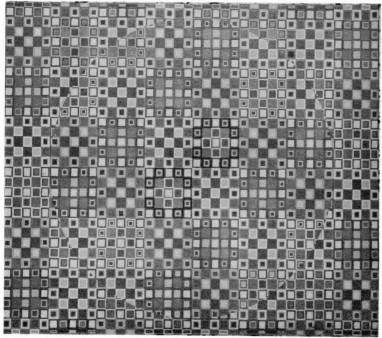

Onosato: *Untitled*. 1964. Oil on canvas, 24 x 28³/₄". Mrs. John D. Rockefeller 3rd, New York.

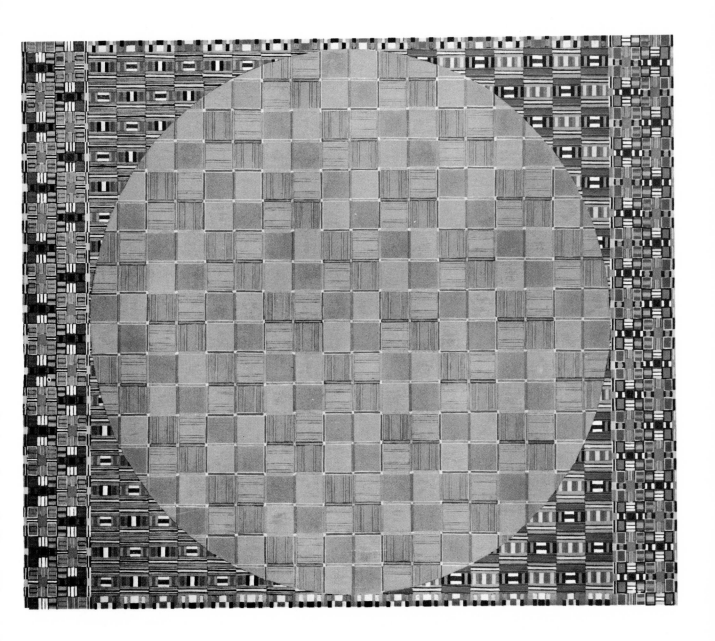

Onosato: *Untitled*. 1961. Oil on canvas, 24 x 28³/₄″. Genmei Ohno, Tokyo.

Nobuya Abe

Born in Niigata City, Niigata Prefecture, 1913. Selt-taught.
1936-1938, traveled in Korea, North China, Manchuria and
Mongolia studying oriental art. Exhibited with first surrealist
group, Bijutsu Bunka Association, 1939-1942, and from 1947,
when it was reorganized, to 1953. In Philippines, 1940,
1943-1946. Elected, 1949, to Executive Committee, Japanese
Artists' Association; organized Japanese representation at
Second International Art Exhibition, New Delhi. Served on
juries of Venice Biennale, São Paulo Bienal, Guggenheim
International Award Exhibition, New York, and other
international exhibitions. On Executive Committee,
International Association of Plastic Arts, 1957; traveled for
it to Germany, France, Spain, Italy, India, Pakistan, Israel
and Yugoslavia, 1957-1962. To U.S.A., 1958, on Leaders' and
Specialists' grant from U.S. State Department. Lives in Rome
and Tokyo. *One-man shows:* Takemiya Gallery, Tokyo, 1952;
Yoseido Gallery, Tokyo; 1955, 1957; Galleria Grattacielo, Milan,
1960; Shirokiya Gallery, Tokyo, 1960; Galleria Alibert, Rome,
1961; Galleria del Cavallino, Venice, 1962; Galleria Cadario,
Milan, 1962; Galleria Naviglio, Milan, 1964. In various group
exhibitions since 1939, including I Bienal, São Paulo, 1951;
Carnegie International Exhibition, Pittsburgh, 1952, 1964;
Second Exhibition of International Art, New Delhi, 1953.
Commissioned to do murals by Ente Nazionale per le
Biblioteche Popolari e Scolastiche, Rome, 1962.

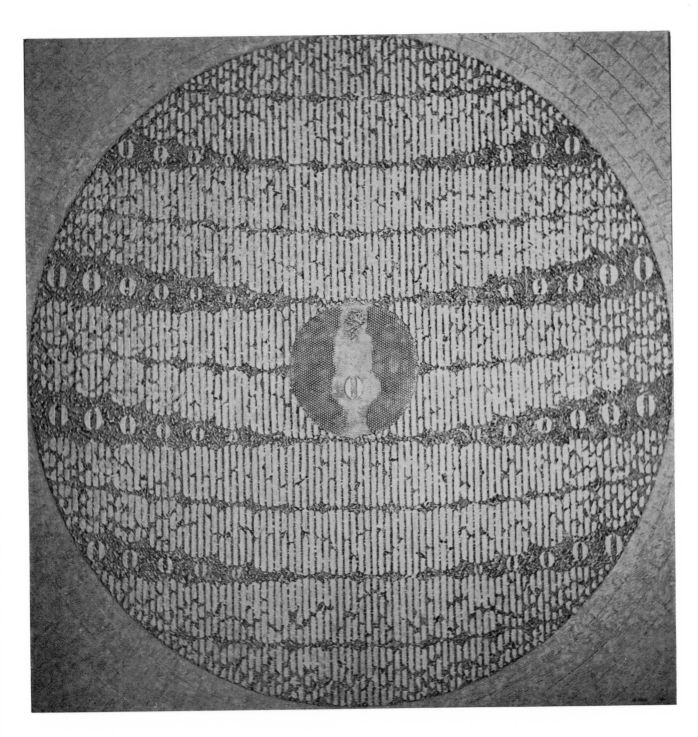

Abe: *Gray Echo*. 1964. Encaustic and canvas on wood, 70½ x 70½″. Mrs. John D. Rockefeller 3rd, New York.

Sei Yamamoto

Born in Okayama City, Okamaya Prefecture, 1915. Studied at
Western Art Center, Tokyo, 1929-1930; Independent Western
Art Center, Tokyo, 1931-1935. Traveled and studied in France,
Italy, Spain, Switzerland, Germany and Belgium, 1956-58.
Lecturer in Art Department, Nippon University, Tokyo, since
1956. Lives in Mitaka City, Tokyo Prefecture. *One-man shows:*
Bungei Shunju Gallery, Tokyo, 1958, 1960-1965 (yearly).
In many group exhibitions in Japan since 1931, including
"Postwar Japanese Artists," National Museum of Modern Art,
Tokyo, 1965. Received Okada Award; Independent Award; Five
City Award. Commissioned by Tokyo Postal Authority to
decorate Postal Authority Building.

Yamamoto: *Sarusawa Pond*. 1964. Oil on canvas, 63⅞ x 51½".
Mrs. John D. Rockefeller 3rd, New York.

Yamamoto: *Yoshino Path*. 1964. Oil on canvas, 51³/₈ x 63³/₄″. Mr. and Mrs. John D. Rockefeller 3rd, New York.

Kazuo Yagi

Born in Kyoto City, Kyoto Prefecture, 1918. Graduated from
Sculpture Department, Kyoto Municipal School of Arts and
Crafts, 1937. Organized Sodeisha group of ceramic artists,
1948. Lecturer, Kyoto Municipal College of Fine Arts, since
1960; Industrial Arts Department, Kyoto Liberal Arts University,
since 1963. Lives in Kyoto. *One-man shows:* Formes
Gallery, Tokyo, 1954; Umeda Gallery, Osaka, 1955; Takemiya
Gallery, Tokyo, 1956; Yoseido Gallery, Tokyo, 1957; Fujikawa
Gallery, Osaka, 1962; Fujikawa Gallery, Tokyo, 1962; Matsuya
Gallery, Tokyo, 1964. Won gold medals at International Ceram-
ics Exhibitions, Ostend, 1959; Prague, 1962. Represented in
collections of University of Michigan, Ann Arbor;
Museum of the City of Kyoto; Museum of Modern Art, New York;
San Francisco Museum of Art.

Yagi: *Queen*. 1964. Black ceramic, 12³/₄″ (including base) x
10¹/₈ x 9⁷/₈″. San Francisco Museum of Art. Gift of
Mrs. Ferdinand C. Smith.

Yagi: *A Cloud Remembered*. 1962. Ceramic, 16″ (including base) x 9³/₄ x 8¹/₄″.
The Museum of Modern Art, New York. Purchase.

Ryokichi Mukai

Born in Kyoto City, Kyoto Prefecture, 1918. Graduated from
Tokyo University of Arts, 1941. Member of Kohdo Art
Association, Tokyo; has exhibited with them since 1948.
Studied in Paris, 1954-1955. Traveled in U.S.A. and Europe,
1958. Lives in Tokyo. In group shows since 1948, including
IV and V Bienal, São Paulo, 1957, 1959; XXXI Biennale, Venice,
1962; "Contemporary Trend of Japanese Paintings and
Sculptures," National Museum of Modern Art, Kyoto, 1964.
Awarded Today's New Artist Prize, 1956; fourth Takamura
Prize, 1961; a prize at VI Biennial, Tokyo, 1961; a prize from
Museum of Modern Art, Kamakura, 1964. Commissioned work
includes wall relief in main hall, and drapery screen, Tokyo
Bunka Kaikan, 1961; decorative windows, Au Printemps, Paris,
1962; monument for Ube City Park, 1963. Represented in
collections of Museum of Modern Art, Kamakura; Museu de
Arte Moderna, São Paulo; National Museum of Modern Art,
Tokyo; Outdoor Museum of Art, Ube.

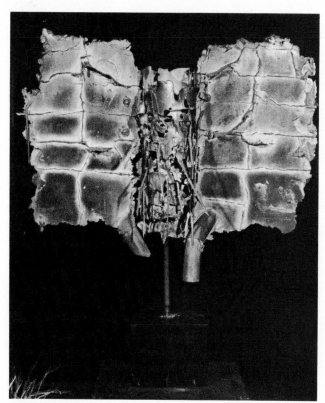

R. Mukai: *The Ants' Castle*. 1960. Cast and welded metal
alloy, 32⅞" (including base) x 29⅝ x 11½". Lent by the artist.

Right, R. Mukai: *The Horse Fly*. 1962. Cast and welded
aluminum, 32½ x 21¼ x 18½". Mrs. John D. Rockefeller 3rd,
New York.

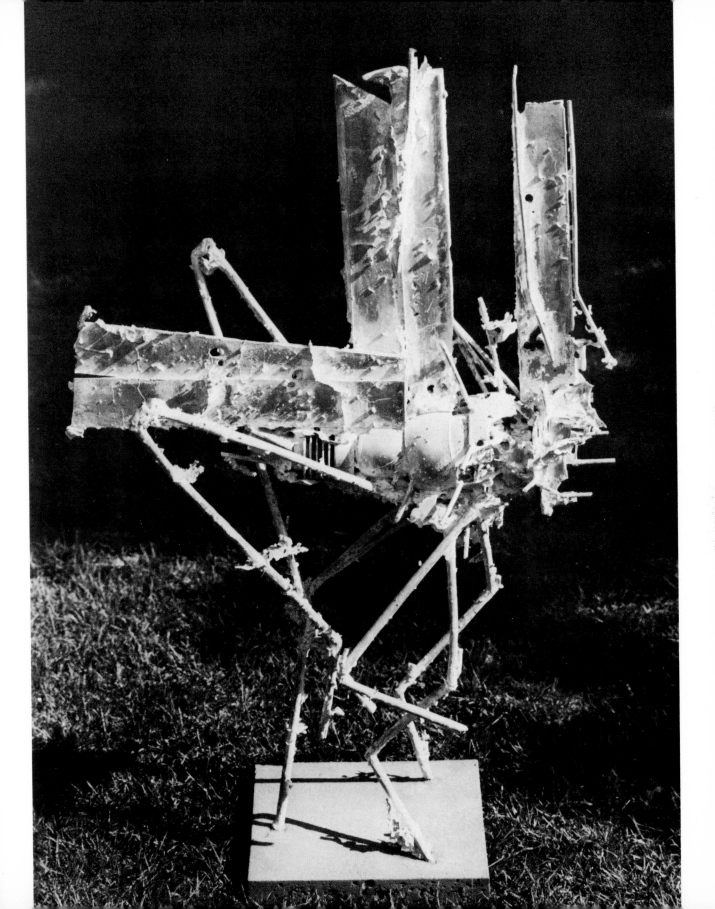

Kakuzo Tatehata

Born in Tokyo, 1919. Sculpture major at Tokyo University
of Arts; graduated 1941. 1941-1943, studied in Research
and Study Department of the University. 1944-1946, in Saigon
for Cultural Institute of Japan; 1953-1955, traveled through
Italy, England, Holland, Belgium and France, spending most
of time in Paris. Since 1959, has taught in Sculpture
Department, Tokyo University of Arts. Lives in Tokyo. In
various group exhibitions in France and Japan since 1940,
including Salon de Mai, Paris, 1954; "Japanese and American
Abstract Artists," National Museum of Modern Art, Tokyo,
1955. Won prizes at Bunten Exhibition, Tokyo, 1941; Mudokai
Exhibition, Tokyo, 1941, 1942. Commissioned to do reliefs for
Riccar Sewing Machine Company Building, Tokyo, 1963; Hotel
New Otani, Tokyo, 1964; Tokyo University of Arts, 1965.

Right, Tatehata: *Gate.* 1964. Cast cement, 69¹/₈ x 46 x 13".
Mrs. Madeleine H. Russell, San Francisco.

Kumi Sugaï

Born in Kobe City, Hyogo Prefecture, 1919. Studied at
Academy of Fine Arts, Osaka, 1927-1932. To Paris, 1952,
where he has lived since. *One-man shows:* Galerie Craven,
Paris, 1954; Palais des Beaux-Arts, Brussels, 1954; Galerie
H. Le Gendre, Paris, 1957; Galerie Creuzevault, Paris, 1958,
1963; Kootz Gallery, New York, 1959-62 (yearly), 1964; Kestner-
Gesellschaft, Hannover, 1963; Die Insel, Hamburg, 1964;
American Art Gallery, Copenhagen, 1965; Konsthallen,
Göteborg, Sweden, 1965; and others. In numerous group
exhibitions since 1953, including Carnegie International
Exhibition, Pittsburgh, 1955, 1958, 1961, 1964; Salon de Mai,
Paris, 1957-1965; V and VIII Bienal, São Paulo, 1959, 1965; II
and III Documenta, Kassel, 1959, 1964; XXXI Biennale, Venice,
1962; "Contemporary Japanese Painting and Sculpture,"
circulated by American Federation of Arts, 1963-64. Awarded
Zagreb Prize, Third International Print Biennial, Ljubljana,
1959; first prize, Tokyo Print Biennial, 1962; first prize, Fourth
International Print Biennial, Ljubljana, 1961; David E. Bright
Foundation Prize for Artists under 45, XXXI Venice Biennale,
1962. Represented in collections of Albright-Knox Art Gallery,
Buffalo, N.Y.; Landesmuseum, Hannover; Atheneum Art
Collection, Helsinki; Kaiser-Wilhelm Museum, Krefeld;
Solomon R. Guggenheim Museum, New York; Museum of
Modern Art, New York; National Museum, Oslo; Carnegie
Institute, Pittsburgh; Museu de Arte Moderna, Rio de Janeiro;
Galleria Nazionale d'Arte Moderna, Rome.

Sugaï: *Oni.* 1956. Oil on canvas, 78³/₄ x 61³/₄″. Mr. and Mrs. Samuel M. Kootz, New York.

Shin Kuno

Born in Nagoya City, Aichi Prefecture, 1921. Studied at Tokyo Higher Normal School, 1940-1943, majoring in art. Enlisted in Naval Air Force, 1944. Has taught in Design Department, Nagoya Industrial Art High School, since 1950. Exhibited with Shinseisaku Association Group, Tokyo, 1952-1960. Lives in Nagoya. *One-man shows:* Muramatsu Gallery, Tokyo, 1957-1960 (yearly); Tokyo Gallery, Tokyo, 1961, 1963; McRoberts and Tunnard Gallery, London, 1963. In many group shows since 1952, including XI Premio Lissone, Lissone (Italy), 1959; Carnegie International Exhibition, Pittsburgh, 1961, 1964; "Adventures in Today's Art of Japan," National Museum of Modern Art, Tokyo, 1961; "Contemporary Japanese Painting and Sculpture," circulated by American Federation of Arts, 1963-64; "Contemporary Japanese Painting," Corcoran Gallery of Art, Washington, D.C., 1964. Awarded Shinseisaku Prize for Young Artists, 1955. Commissioned to do mural in Zenkyoren Building, Tokyo, 1963. Represented in collection of Museum of Contemporary Art, Nagaoka.

52

Kuno: *Untitled.* 1963. Lacquered steel relief mounted on wood, 50⅛ x 35⅞ x 1¾". Mrs. John D. Rockefeller 3rd, New York.

Kuno: *Untitled*. 1961. Lacquered steel relief mounted on wood, 50⅛ x 35⅞ x 2⅛".
Lent anonymously.

Hiroshi Akana

Born in Nemuro City, Nemuro Prefecture (Hokkaido Island), 1922. Graduated from Department of Graphic Design, Tokyo College of Industrial Arts, 1943. Has taught in Design Department, Chiba University, Tokyo, since 1946. Has exhibited with Shinseisaku Association, Tokyo, since 1947; became a member, 1956. Lives in Tokyo. *One-man shows:* Takemiya Gallery, Tokyo, 1951; Nabisu Gallery, Tokyo, 1955; Hiroshi Gallery, Tokyo, 1958; Tokyo Gallery, Tokyo, 1961. In various group exhibitions since 1947, including 18th International Water Color Exhibition, Brooklyn Museum, Brooklyn, N.Y., 1955; "Contemporary New Artist Exhibition," Museum of Modern Art, Kamakura, 1956. Awarded prizes by Shinseisaku Association, 1949, 1950, 1955; Sakura Gallery, Tokyo, 1953. Represented in collections of Museum of Contemporary Art, Nagaoka; National Museum of Modern Art, Tokyo.

Akana: *Pair*. 1963. Oil on canvas, 71³/₄ x 89¹/₂". Lent by the artist.

Left, Akana: *Fighting Spirit*. 1964. Oil on canvas, 71¹/₂ x 89³/₄". Lent by the artist.

Shigeru Izumi

Born in Osaka City, Osaka Prefecture, 1922. Lived in New York, 1959-1962, under sponsorship of Japan Society; taught at Pratt Institute, Brooklyn, N. Y. 1962, to Paris, where he now lives. *One-man shows:* Hankyu Gallery, Osaka, 1949; Umeda Gallery, Osaka, 1951, 1957, 1964; Matsushima Gallery, Tokyo, 1952; Takemiya Gallery, Tokyo, 1953, 1954, 1957; Minami Gallery, Tokyo, 1958; Pratt Institute, Brooklyn, N.Y., 1959; Mi Chou Gallery, New York, 1962. In various group exhibitions, including IV Bienal, São Paulo, 1957; "30 Peintres et 6 Sculpteurs de l'Ecole de Paris," Musée des Beaux-Arts, Nantes, 1963. Awarded prizes at Tokyo International Print Biennials, 1957, 1961. Represented in collections of New York University, New York; Riverside Museum, New York; Rockefeller Foundation, New York; Musée National d'Art Moderne, Paris; Carnegie Institute, Pittsburgh; National Museum of Modern Art, Tokyo.

Below, Izumi: *Painting.* 1964. Oil on canvas, 35 x 45³/₄".
Mrs. John D. Rockefeller 3rd, New York.

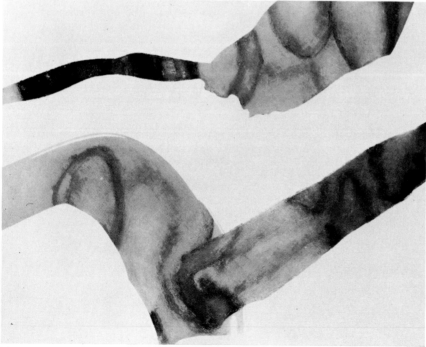

Izumi: *Painting.* 1965. Oil on canvas, 44⅞ x 57½″. Galerie Suzanne De Coninck, Paris.

Soichiro Tomioka

Born in Takada City, Niigata Prefecture, 1922. Studied business at Takada High School, 1934-1939. Studied art privately. Has exhibited with Shinseisaku Association, Tokyo, since 1953. Art Director, Mitsubishi Chemical Industries, 1953-1965. Visited U.S.A. (New York, San Francisco and Hawaii), 1963. Lives in Tokyo. *One-man shows:* Kabutoya Gallery, Tokyo, 1958; Takegawa Gallery, Tokyo, 1959, 1961; Nihonbashi Gallery, Tokyo, 1962, 1963; Nihonbashi Gallery, New York, 1963. In many group shows, including the VII Bienal, São Paulo, 1963; "Contemporary Japanese Painting," Corcoran Gallery of Art, Washington, D. C., 1964. Won Shinseisaku Association Prize, 1961, 1962; prize in Contemporary Japanese Art Exhibition, Tokyo, 1962; Caio Alcantara Machado Prize, São Paulo, 1963. Commissioned to do work for Mitsubishi Exhibition Center, Tokyo; joint work with Kenmochi Design Association. Represented in collections of Museu de Arte Moderna, São Paulo; National Museum of Modern Art, Tokyo.

Tomioka: *Untitled*. August, 1964. Oil on canvas, 64 x 63¾". Lent by the artist.

Tomioka: *Untitled*. May, 1964. Oil on canvas, 63⅞ x 63¾″. Mrs. Bliss Parkinson, New York.

Sadamasa Motonaga

Born in Ueno City, Mie Prefecture, 1922. Graduated from Ueno Commercial High School, 1938. Studied under Mankichi Hamabe, 1946-1952. Moved to Kobe City, Hyogo Prefecture, 1952. In 1955, became student of Jiro Yoshihara and member of Gutai Art Association, Osaka, exhibiting with latter since then. Lives in Takarazuka City, Hyogo Prefecture. *One-man shows:* Martha Jackson Gallery, New York, 1961; Tokyo Gallery, Tokyo, 1961, 1963; Yamada Gallery, Kyoto, 1965. In many group shows since 1955, including XI and XII Premio Lissone, Lissone (Italy), 1959, 1961; "Four Japanese Artists," Martha Jackson Gallery, New York, 1960; "Adventure in Today's Art of Japan," National Museum of Modern Art, Tokyo, 1961; "Contemporary Japanese Painting," Corcoran Gallery of Art, Washington, D.C., 1964. Awarded prizes at Premio Lissone, 1959; Tokyo Contemporary Art Exhibition, 1964; received Contemporary Art Award of Kobe, 1964. Represented in collections of Museum of Contemporary Art, Nagaoka; Gutai Pinacotheca, Osaka; National Museum of Modern Art, Tokyo.

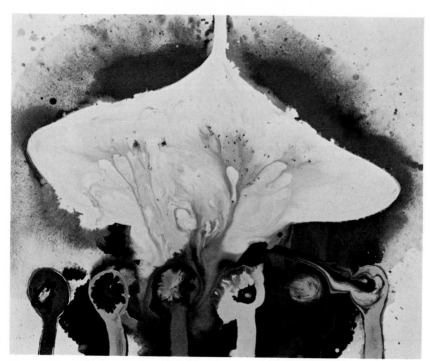

Motonaga: *Untitled.* 1964. Oil on canvas, 36¹/₈ x 45⁵/₈". Lent anonymously.

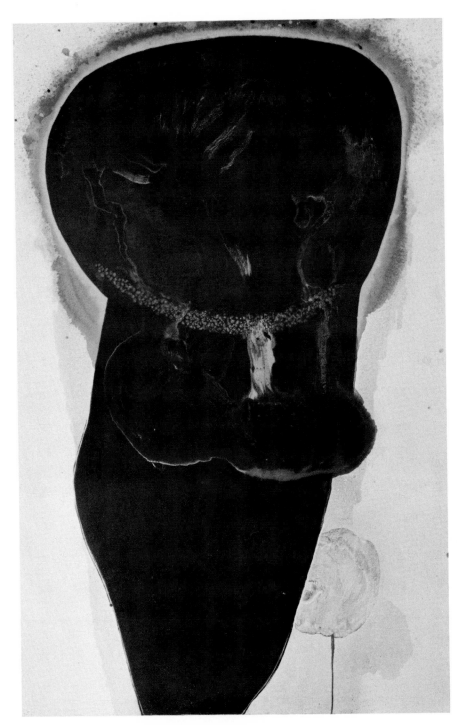

Motonaga: *Untitled*. 1964. Oil on canvas, 108¼ x 70¼". Lent by the artist.

Masayuki Nagare

Born in Nagasaki City, Nagasaki Prefecture, 1923. Studied at Ritsumeikan University, Kyoto, 1941-1943. In Naval Air Force, 1943-1946. Is architect and sculptor. Lives on island of Shikoku. *One-man shows:* Tokyo, 1952, 1954, 1957; Staempfli Gallery, New York, 1963. In various group exhibitions, including Carnegie International Exhibition, Pittsburgh, 1961, 1964; "Contemporary Japanese Painting and Sculpture," circulated by American Federation of Arts, 1963-64. Received Japan Architectural Award, 1963. Commissioned work includes gardens and fountains, Palace Hotel, Tokyo, 1964; sculpture gardens and fountains, Ueno Festival Hall, Tokyo, 1962; sculptured stone walls, Japanese Pavilion, New York World's Fair, 1964-65. Represented in collection of Museum of Modern Art, New York.

Nagare: *Windwoven.* 1962. Granite, 11¼ x 28⅜ x 19¼".
Mrs. Emily B. Staempfli, New York.

Nagare: *Plowing.* 1958. Granite, 14¼ x 12¼ x 10⅜".
Mr. and Mrs. Robert M. Benjamin, New York.

Nagare: *Enclosure.* 1959. Granite, 8½ x 22¾ x 17". Mrs. John D. Rockefeller 3rd, New York.

Kazuo Shiraga

Born in Amagasaki City, Hyogo Prefecture, 1924. Studied
traditional painting at Tokyo Municipal Art School,
1942-1948. 1948, began to study under Jiro Yoshihara. Became
member of Gutai Art Association, Osaka, 1955; has exhibited
with them since. 1957-1960, taught at Amagasaki Municipal
Seibun Primary School. Lives in Amagasaki. *One-man shows:*
Galerie Stadler, Paris, 1962; Tokyo Gallery, Tokyo, 1962, 1964;
International Center of Aesthetic Research, Turin, 1962;
Galleria Notizie, Turin, 1962; Gutai Pinacotheca, Osaka, 1962.
In many group exhibitions in Japan and abroad since 1955,
including XI Premio Lissone, Lissone (Italy), 1959; "Adventure
in Today's Art of Japan," National Museum of Modern Art,
Tokyo, 1961. Awarded prizes at XI Premio Lissone, 1959; VIII
Biennial, Tokyo, 1965. Represented in collection of Museum
of Contemporary Art, Nagaoka.

Shiraga: *Untitled*. 1964. Oil on canvas,
51½ x 76⅜". Lent anonymously.

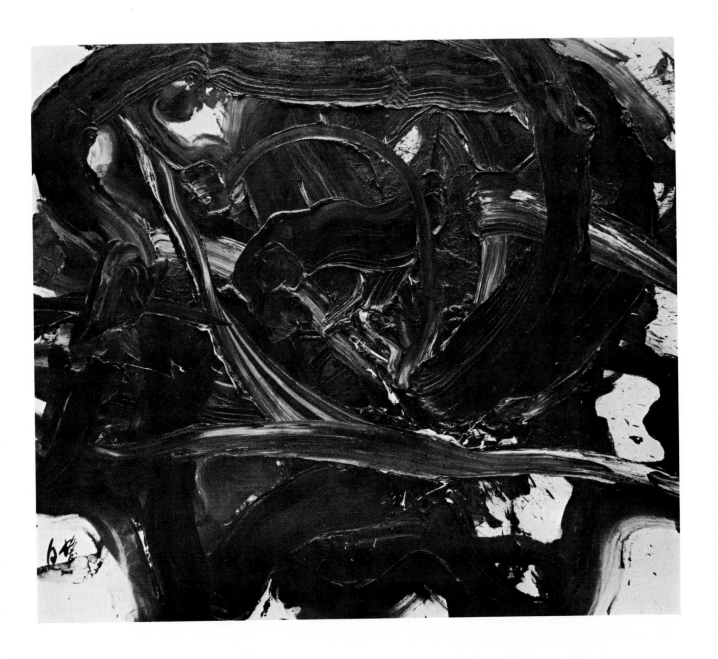

Shiraga: *Untitled*. 1964. Oil on canvas, 85½ x 95⅝″. The Museum of Contemporary Art, Nagaoka.

Tomonori Toyofuku

Born in Kurume City, Fukuoka Prefecture, 1925. Graduated
from Kokugakuin University, Tokyo, 1943, with degree in
ancient Japanese literature. Studied wood sculpture under
Chiodo Tominaga, 1946-1948. Exhibited with Shinseisaku
Association, Tokyo, 1950-1957; became a member, 1957.
Since 1960, has lived in Milan. *One-man shows:* Tokyo Gallery,
Tokyo, 1960; Drian Gallery, London, 1962; Galleria Grattacielo,
Milan, 1962; Galleria del Cavallino, Venice, 1962; Galleria
Naviglio, Milan, 1963, 1965; George Lester Gallery, Rome, 1963.
In various international group shows, including XXX and
XXXII Biennale, Venice, 1960, 1964; Carnegie International
Exhibition, Pittsburgh, 1964; VIII Bienal, São Paulo, 1965
(invited). Awarded Takamura Prize for Distinguished Sculpture,
1959; third prize, International Competition of Architecture and
Art, Copenhagen, 1961; William Frew Memorial Purchase
Prize, Carnegie International Exhibition, Pittsburgh, 1964.
Represented in collections of Atheneum Art Collection,
Helsinki; Museum of Modern Art, New York; National Museum
of Modern Art, Tokyo.

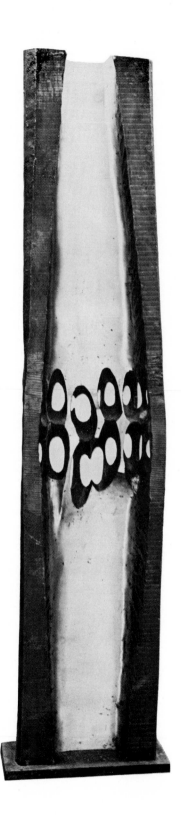

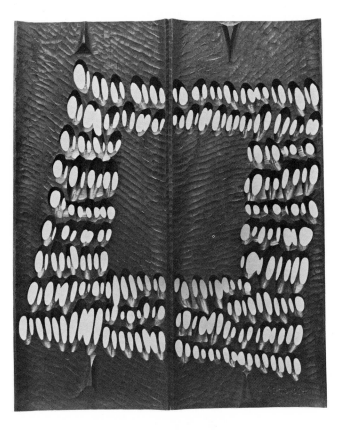

Above, Toyofuku: *Ventus.* 1964. Wood, 55³/₈ x 45¼".
Mr. and Mrs. Robert W. Sarnoff, New York.

Right, Toyofuku: *Adrift, III.* 1960. Wood, 83⁷/₈ x 120 x 33".
The Museum of Modern Art, New York. Philip C. Johnson Fund.

Left, Toyofuku: *Sui, III.* 1964. Bronze, 80¹/₈ x 19 x 9⁷/₈".
Joseph H. Hirshhorn Collection, New York.

Kengiro Azuma

Born in Yamagata City, Yamagata Prefecture, 1926. Studied sculpture at Tokyo Academy of Fine Arts, 1949-1954. Exhibited with Shinseisaku Association, Tokyo, 1953-1955. Assistant in sculpture, Tokyo Academy, 1955-1956. In Italy, 1956-1960, on scholarship from Italian government; studied at Brera Academy, Milan, under Marino Marini. Lives in Milan. *One-man shows:* Galleria Minima, Milan, 1961, 1962; Galleria dell' Obelisco, Rome, 1962; Galleria del Cavallino, Venice, 1962; Toninelli Arte Moderna, Milan, 1963; Galerie Falazik, Bochum (Germany), 1964; Galerie Emmy Widmann, Bremen, 1964; Galleria Flaviana, Locarno, 1964; Galerie Senatore, Stuttgart, 1964; Galleria Meridiana, Biella (Italy), 1965; Galleria Giraldi, Leghorn, 1965; and others. In numerous group exhibitions since 1953, including "Arte e Contemplazione," Palazzo Grassi, Venice, 1961; Third International Sculpture Exhibition, State Town Hall, Carrara, 1962; International Sculpture Exhibition, State Museum for Modern Art, Taipei, 1963; III Documenta, Kassel, 1964. Awarded Prix Emile Godard, International Sculpture Exhibition, Lausanne, 1963; first prize, VII Biennial, Tokyo, 1963; second prize, Fifth International Bronzetto Exhibition, Padua, 1963; Takamura Prize for Best Japanese Sculptor of 1963, Tokyo, 1964; second prize, XII International Sculpture Contest, Monza, 1964. Represented in collection of National Museum of Modern Art, Tokyo.

Azuma: *MU S-56.* 1962. Bronze, 22⅛" (including base) x 12¼". Toninelli Arte Moderna, Milan.

Azuma: *MU S-116*. 1963. Bronze, 30⅝ x 18¼ x 9¼". Toninelli Arte Moderna, Milan.

Reiji Kimura

Born in Tokyo, 1926. Graduated from Chiba University, Tokyo, 1948. Taught high school art courses, Tokyo, 1948-1954. Exhibited in Tokyo with Jiyu Art Association, 1952; with Nika Association, 1953-1955. To U.S.A. 1956; lives in New York. *One-man shows:* YMCA, Honolulu, Hawaii, 1957; The Print Club, Philadelphia, 1962. In various group shows since 1958, including Kane Memorial Exhibition, "Contemporary Master Drawings and Prints," Providence, R.I., 1963.

Kimura: *No. S.A.* 1964. Oil and metal paint on paper and composition board, 15½ x 14⅜". George Montgomery, New York.

Kimura: *No. 164.* 1964. Oil and metal paint on paper and canvas, 72⁵/₈ x 52¹/₂″. Lent by the artist.

71

Katsuhiro Yamaguchi

Born in Tokyo, 1928. Studied law at Nihon University, Tokyo, 1949-1952. Traveled to Italy, Spain and New York City, 1961-62. Lives in Tokyo. *One-man shows:* Matsushima Gallery, Tokyo, 1952; Takemiya Gallery, Tokyo, 1953; American Cultural Center, Yokohama, 1955; Sato Gallery, Tokyo, 1961; Akiyama Gallery, Tokyo, 1964. In various group exhibitions in Japan since 1953, including "Abstraction and Surrealism," National Museum of Modern Art, Tokyo, 1953; "Japanese and American Abstract Artists," National Museum of Modern Art, Tokyo, 1955; "Artists Today," Yokohama City Gallery, Yokohama, 1964. Commissioned to do glass murals for United States Atomic Power Pavilion, International Trade Fair, Tokyo, 1957; Wako Department Store, Tokyo, 1958.

K. Yamaguchi: *Jet.* 1964. Cloth stretched over metal wire, 65 x 79 x 42½". Lent by the artist.

Hisao Domoto

Born in Kyoto City, Kyoto Prefecture, 1928. Studied traditional Japanese painting, Kyoto Academy of Fine Arts, 1945-1949. Exhibited at Salon de l'Académie, Tokyo, for several years. Traveled to France, Italy and Spain, 1952. In 1956, moved to Paris, where he now lives. *One-man shows:* Galerie Stadler, Paris, 1957, 1959, 1962; Galerie Schmela, Düsseldorf, 1958; Galleria Notizie, Turin, 1958; Galerie Nebelung, Düsseldorf, 1959; Martha Jackson Gallery, New York, 1959; Galleria Il Segno, Rome, 1959; Minami Gallery, Tokyo, 1960; Nitta Gallery, Tokyo, 1961; Galerie Handschin, Basel, 1963; Galleria Pogliani, Rome, 1963; Rotterdamsche Kunstkring, Rotterdam, 1964; Galerie Europe, Paris, 1965. In various group exhibitions since 1948, including Salon de Mai, Paris, 1956, 1957, 1962; "Young Foreign Artists," Musée National d'Art Moderne, Paris, 1958; XI and XII Premio Lissone, Lissone (Italy), 1959, 1961; Carnegie International Exhibition, Pittsburgh, 1960, 1961, 1964; Guggenheim International Award Exhibition, New York, 1961; VI Bienal, São Paulo, 1961; "Strutture e Stile," Museo Civico d'Arte Moderna, Milan, 1962; XXXII Biennale, Venice, 1964. Awarded first prize, Salon de l'Académie, Tokyo, 1951, 1953; first prize, "Young Foreign Artists," Musée National d'Art Moderne, Paris, 1958; Chalette Prize, XXXII Biennale, Venice, 1964. Represented in collections of Albright-Knox Art Gallery, Buffalo, N.Y.; Kunstverein, Cologne; Museum of Fine Arts, Houston, Texas; Museum of the City of Kyoto; Museum of Modern Art, New York; Musée National d'Art Moderne, Paris; Galleria Nazionale d'Arte Moderna, Rome; National Museum of Modern Art, Tokyo; Galleria Civica d'Arte Moderna, Turin.

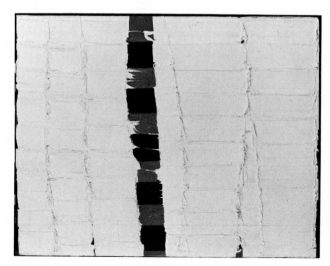

Domoto: *Solution of Continuity, 22.* 1964. Oil on canvas, 38⅛ x 51". Howard E. Johnson, Oakland, California.

Domoto: *Solution of Continuity, 24.* 1964. Oil on canvas, 63⅝ x 51⅛". The Museum of Modern Art, New York. Gift of Mr. and Mrs. David Kluger.

Takeshi Kawashima

Born in Takamatsu City, Kagawa Prefecture, 1930. Studied at
Musashino Art School, Tokyo, 1953-1955. Taught at Yoyogi Art
School, Tokyo, 1955-1958. Exhibited with Yomiuri Independ-
ents, Tokyo, 1961-1963. To U.S.A., 1963; lives in New York.
One-man shows: Muramatsu Gallery, Tokyo, 1958-1961 (yearly).
Commissioned to do mural for Agricultural Hall, Takamatsu,
1963. Represented in collections of Museum of Modern Art,
Kyobashi; Museum of Modern Art, New York; National
Museum, Tokyo.

Opposite, Kawashima: *Untitled 1964, New York.* Center panel of a triptych. 1964. Oil on canvas,
100½ x 80″. The Museum of Modern Art, New York. Purchase. Below, the triptych: right panel,
collection of Mr. and Mrs. Frederick R. Weisman, Beverly Hills; left panel, Mr. and Mrs. Samuel
J. Zacks, Toronto.

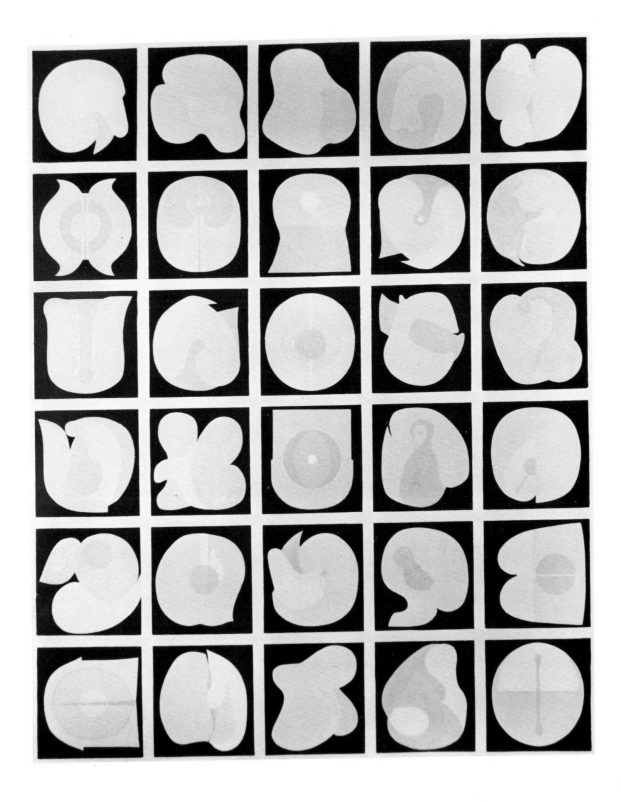

Minoru Niizuma

Born in Tokyo, 1930. Graduated from Tokyo University of Arts, 1955. Exhibited with Modern Art Association, Tokyo, 1954-1958; elected permanent jury member, 1957. Taught sculpture and drawing at Seijo School, Tokyo, 1955-1958. To U.S.A., 1959; Lives in New York. Has taught sculpture at Brooklyn Museum Art School since 1964. *One-man shows:* Takemiya Gallery, Tokyo, 1955; Muramatsu Gallery, Tokyo, 1957; Fugetsudo Gallery, Tokyo, 1958; Sato Gallery, Tokyo, 1958. In various group shows in Japan including "Shuro Sculpture Show," Matsuzakaya Gallery, Tokyo, 1957-1958. Commissioned to make monument for city of Tokyo, 1956; monument for Asia Center, Tokyo, 1958. Represented in collection of Museum of Modern Art, New York.

Niizuma: *Castle of the Eye.* 1964. Marble, 18½ x 15¾ x 8".
The Museum of Modern Art, New York. Purchase.

Niizuma: *The Waves' Voice.* 1963. Granite, 27⅞ x 20½ x 5″. Mrs. John D. Rockefeller 3rd, New York.

Morio Shinoda

Born in Tokyo, 1931. Attended Aoyama University, Tokyo, 1950-1954; majored in English literature. Since 1952, has worked as designer at Industrial Arts Institute, Tokyo; since 1958, has taught night classes at Tokyo Design School. Visited U.S.A., 1963-1964. Lives in Tokyo. In many group shows in Japan, including "New Generation of Japanese Sculptors," National Museum of Modern Art, Tokyo, 1963; "Contemporary Trend of Japanese Paintings and Sculptures," National Museum of Modern Art, Kyoto, 1964; "First Exhibition for the Prize of the Nagaoka Museum," Museum of Contemporary Art, Nagaoka, 1964. Awarded first prize by Modern Art Association, Tokyo, 1956. Represented in collections of Museum of Modern Art, Kamakura; Museum of Contemporary Art, Nagaoka.

Shinoda: *Tension and Compression*. 1960. Bronze and wire, 19 x 15³/₈ x 7¹/₄". Lent anonymously.

Shinoda: *Tension and Compression*. 1962. Bronze and wire, 26⅞ x 33 x 23⅞″. Mrs. John D. Rockefeller 3rd, New York.

Shyu Eguchi

Born in Kyoto City, Kyoto Prefecture, 1932. Entered Tokyo University of Arts, 1951; graduated from Sculpture Department, 1956. Has taught at Women's Junior College of Arts, Tokyo, since 1963. Traveled to Hong Kong, 1964. Lives in Fuchu City, Tokyo Prefecture. *One-man show:* Akiyama Gallery, Tokyo, 1964. In various group shows since 1957, including "New Generation of Japanese Sculptors," National Museum of Modern Art, Tokyo, 1963; "Contemporary Trend of Japanese Paintings and Sculptures," National Museum of Modern Art, Kyoto, 1964. Represented in collection of Museum of Modern Art, New York.

Eguchi: *Monument No. 1.* 1963. Cherry, 41³/₈ x 17 x 20³/₈″. Mrs. Gilbert W. Chapman, New York.

Eguchi: *Monument No. 4.* 1964. Cherry, 18¼ x 22 x 14¼″. The Museum of Modern Art, New York. Purchase.

Masanobu Yoshimura

Born in Oita City, Oita Prefecture, 1932. Studied at Musashino
Art School, Tokyo, 1951-1955. Taught painting to children,
1952-1960. Exhibited with Yomiuri Independents, Tokyo,
1955-1962. To U.S.A., 1962; lives in New York. *One-man shows:*
Muramatsu Gallery, Tokyo, 1955, 1961; Chuo Gallery, Tokyo,
1957; Sato Gallery, Tokyo, 1960; Fugetsudo Gallery, Tokyo,
1962. In numerous group exhibitions since 1955 in Japan and
New York. Awarded third prize, Shell Award Exhibitions,
Tokyo, 1959, 1960. Represented in collection of Museum of
Modern Art, New York.

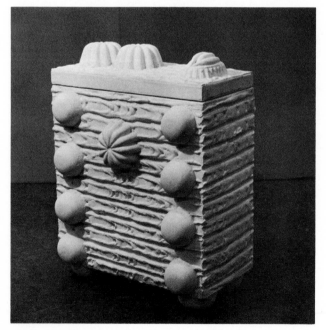

Yoshimura: *Coffer.* 1963. Plaster on wood, with canvas interior,
32 x 25½ x 17½". Lent by the artist.

Yoshimura: *Two Columns*. 1964. Plaster on wood, with base and plexiglas vitrine. 74¼″ (including base) x 36 x 17⅞″. The Museum of Modern Art, New York. Purchase.

Atsuko Tanaka

Born in Osaka City, Osaka Prefecture, 1932. Graduated from
Shoin Senior High School, Osaka, 1950. Attended Kyoto
Municipal College of Fine Arts, 1951; later studied under Jiro
Yoshihara. Became a member of Gutai Art Association, Osaka,
1955; has exhibited in all their shows since. Lives in Osaka.
One-man shows: Gutai Pinacotheca, Osaka, 1963; Minami
Gallery, Tokyo, 1963. In many group shows since 1955,
including Guggenheim International Award Exhibition,
New York, 1960, 1964; Carnegie International Exhibition,
Pittsburgh, 1961; "Adventure in Today's Art of Japan," National
Museum of Modern Art, Tokyo, 1961; "First Exhibition for
the Prize of the Nagaoka Museum," Museum of Contemporary
Art, Nagaoka, 1964. Won prize at Contemporary Japanese Art
Exhibition, Tokyo, 1964. Commissioned to do window
decoration in lobby of Art Printing Company Building, Tokyo,.
1963; watercolor for Hideji Kogai of I.B.M. Company, Japan,
1964. Represented in collection of the Museum of
Contemporary Art, Nagaoka; Museum of Modern Art, New York.

Tanaka: *Untitled*. 1964. Vinyl on canvas, 77¼ x 52″. Minami Gallery, Tokyo.

Masaaki Kusumoto

Born in Nagano City, Nagano Prefecture, 1933. Studied traditional Japanese painting at Tokyo University of Arts, 1952-1956.
Art Director, Morinaga Miki Industry, 1957-1961. To U.S.A.,
1961; lives in New York. *One-man shows:* Mimatsu Gallery,
Tokyo, 1958; Muramatsu Gallery, Tokyo, 1959. In various group
shows in Japan since 1956.

Kusumoto: *Environment and Movement.* 1964. Synthetic polymer paint and metal foil on canvas, 110¼ x 120⅛″. Lent by the artist.

Shinjiro Okamoto

Born in Tokyo, 1933. Graduated from Tokyo Nihonbashi High School, 1952. Exhibited with Yomiuri Independents, Tokyo, 1956-1963. Lives in Tokyo; works in design section, Toppan Printing Company. *One-man shows;* Muramatsu Gallery, Tokyo, 1956; Kunugi Gallery, Tokyo, 1962, 1963; Mudo Gallery, Tokyo, 1964; Sakura Gallery, Tokyo, 1965; Yoshida Gallery, Tokyo, 1965. In group shows in Japan since 1956, including "Contemporary Trend of Japanese Paintings and Sculptures," National Museum of Modern Art, Kyoto, 1964; "First Exhibition for the Prize of the Nagaoka Museum," Museum of Contemporary Art, Nagaoka, 1964; "Young Seven," Minami Gallery, Tokyo, 1964. Won prizes at Niki Exhibition, Tokyo, 1958; Shell Award Exhibitions, Tokyo, 1962, 1963; received Art Publishing Award, International Young Artists Exhibition, Tokyo, and Nagaoka Museum Award, 1964. Represented in collection of Museum of Contemporary Art, Nagaoka.

Okamoto: *Ninth Little Indian.* 1964. Acrylic on canvas, 57½ x 38¼". Mrs. Robert F. Windfohr, Fort Worth, Texas.

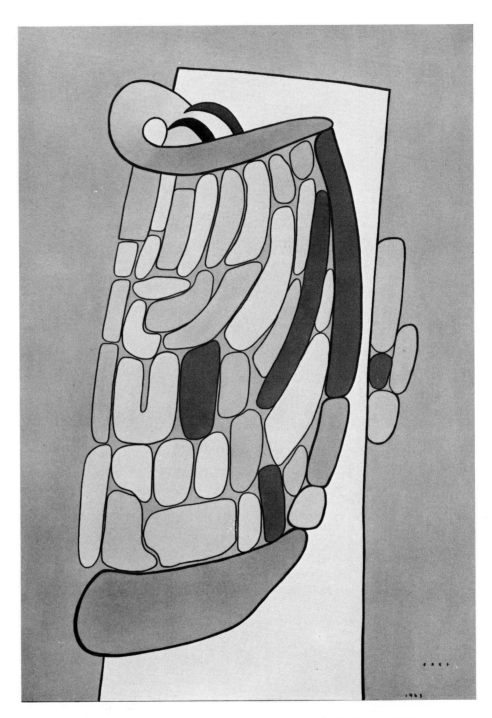

Okamoto: *The Big Laugh*. 1963. Acrylic on canvas, 63⅞ x 44¼". Mrs. Robert F. Windfohr, Fort Worth, Texas.

Tadasky (Tadasuke Kuwayama)

Born in Nagoya City, Aichi Prefecture, 1935. Self-taught. To U.S.A., 1961; lives in New York. *One-man show:* Kootz Gallery, New York, 1965. In group shows in U.S.A., including "The Responsive Eye," Museum of Modern Art, New York, 1965. Represented in collections of Albright-Knox Art Gallery, Buffalo, N.Y.; Museum of Modern Art, New York; "Old Hundred," Larry Aldrich Museum, Ridgefield, Conn.

Tadasky: *T-104*. 1965. Acrylic on canvas, 68 x 68″. Kootz Gallery, New York.

Mokuma Kikuhata

Born in Nagasaki City, Nagasaki Prefecture, 1935. Studied at
Fukuoka Prefectural Central High School, 1950-1953. Exhibited
with Yomiuri Independents, Tokyo, 1958-1960. Lives in Fukuoka
City, Fukuoka Prefecture. *One-man shows:* Minami Gallery,
Tokyo, 1962, 1964. In various group shows since 1958, including
"Adventure in Today's Art of Japan," National Museum of
Modern Art, Tokyo, 1961; "Contemporary Trend of Japanese
Paintings and Sculptures," National Museum of Modern Art,
Kyoto, 1964; "Young Seven," Minami Gallery, Tokyo, 1964.
Won Stralem Award, International Young Artists Exhibition,
Tokyo, 1964. Now working on commission from architect
Shinichiro Yoshihara to decorate exterior wall of Kanagawa
Prefectural Electricity Hall. Represented in collection of
Museum of Modern Art, New York.

Kikuhata: *Roulette: Target*. 1964. Enamel paint and assemblage
on wood, 48 x 33¼ x 6⅛". Lent anonymously.

94

Kikuhata: *Roulette: Ancient Shield*. 1964. Enamel paint and assemblage on wood, 38³/₈ x 31¹/₈ x 4³/₄".
Mrs. John D. Rockefeller 3rd, New York.

Nobuaki Kojima

Born in Ono City, Fukui Prefecture, 1935. Graduated from Fine Arts Department, Osaka City Arts High School, 1955. Exhibited with Yomiuri Independents, Tokyo, 1958-1963. Lives in Tokyo. *One-man shows:* Muramatsu Gallery, Tokyo, 1962; Tsubaki Modern Gallery, Tokyo, 1964. In various group shows in Japan since 1963, including "Contemporary Trend of Japanese Paintings and Sculptures," National Museum of Modern Art, Kyoto, 1965.

Right, Kojima: *Untitled.* 1964. Originally created as shown on opposite page. Work partially destroyed in 1964. See catalog for remaining figures.

Natsuyuki Nakanishi

Born in Tokyo, 1935. Majored in painting at Tokyo University of Arts, 1954-1958. Taught elementary school, 1958-1963. Lives in Tokyo. *One-man shows:* Kunugi Gallery, Tokyo, 1958; Muramatsu Gallery, Tokyo, 1958; Ito Gallery, Tokyo, 1960. In various group shows since 1959, including "Adventure in Today's Art of Japan," National Museum of Modern Art, Tokyo, 1961; "New Generation of Japanese Sculptors," National Museum of Modern Art, Tokyo, 1963; "Contemporary Trend of Japanese Paintings and Sculptures," National Museum of Modern Art, Kyoto, 1964; "First Exhibition for the Prize of the Nagaoka Museum," Museum of Contemporary Art, Nagaoka, 1964. Represented in collections of Museum of Contemporary Art, Nagaoka; Museum of Modern Art, New York.

Right, Nakanishi: *Compact Objects (6).* 1962. Assemblages contained in polyester, each 9 x 5⅞ x 5⅞". Lent by the artist; Mrs. John D. Rockefeller 3rd, New York; Mrs. Warren Tremaine, Santa Barbara, California; and The Museum of Modern Art, New York (Purchase).

Left, Nakanishi: *Compact Object.* Assemblage contained in polyester, 9 x 5⅞ x 5⅞".

Shusaku Arakawa

Born in Nagoya City, Aichi Prefecture, 1936. Lived in Tokyo, 1959-1962. Associated briefly with Yomiuri Independents, Tokyo, and Neo-Dada Group, Tokyo. To U.S.A., 1962; lives in New York. *One-man shows:* Muramatsu Gallery, Tokyo, 1959; Galerie Schmela, Düsseldorf, 1963, 1965; Palais des Beaux-Arts, Brussels, 1964; Dwan Gallery, Los Angeles, 1964; Minami Gallery, Tokyo, 1965. In various group shows since 1960, including "Contemporary Trend of Japanese Paintings and Sculptures," National Museum of Modern Art, Kyoto, 1964; "Young Seven," Minami Gallery, Tokyo, 1964.

Below, Arakawa: *Card into Feather, Eternal Magic.* 1964. Oil on canvas, 63¼ x 91". Mrs. John D. Rockefeller 3rd, New York.

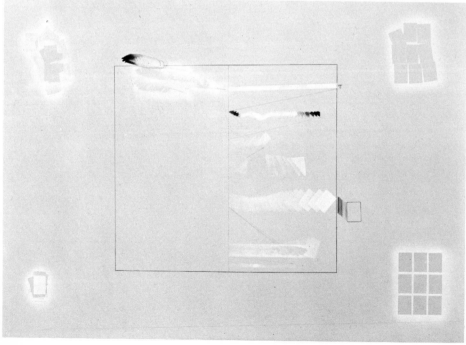

100

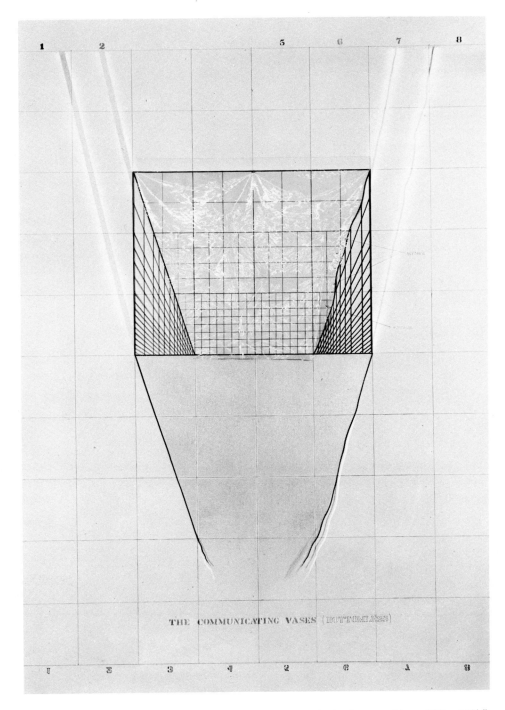

Arakawa: *The Communicating Vases*. 1965. Oil on canvas with plastic assemblage, 89³/₈ x 63⁷/₈″.
Dwan Gallery, Los Angeles.

Yukihisa Isobe

Born in Tokyo, 1936. Studied at Tokyo University of Arts,
1952-1956. Exhibited with Yomiuri Independents, Tokyo, 1962,
1963. Traveled in Europe and U.S.A., 1956, 1965. Lives in Tokyo.
One-man shows: Tokyo Gallery, Tokyo, 1962, 1964, 1965;
Galleria del Cavallino, Venice, 1965. In various group shows
since 1962, including VII Bienal, São Paulo, 1963;
"Contemporary Trend of Japanese Paintings and Sculptures,"
National Museum of Modern Art, Kyoto, 1964; "Contemporary
Japanese Painting," Corcoran Gallery of Art, Washington, D.C.,
1964; "First Exhibition for the Prize of the Nagaoka Museum,"
Museum of Contemporary Art, Nagaoka, 1964. Awarded prize
for prints, VII Biennial, Tokyo, 1963; Purchase Prize, Museum
of Contemporary Art, Nagaoka, 1964. Commissioned to do
mural for Zenkyoren Building, Tokyo, 1963; architectural
design and sculpture for Negishi Pool Center, Yokohama, 1964.
Represented in collections of Museum of Contemporary Art,
Nagaoka; National Museum of Modern Art, Tokyo.

Isobe: *Untitled*. 1964. Assemblage, 71³/₄ x 71¹/₂ x 2¹/₂". Brooks Walker, San Francisco.

Hisayuki Mogami

Born in Yokosuka City, Kanagawa Prefecture, 1936. Entered
Tokyo University of Arts, 1956; graduated from Sculpture
Department, 1960. Exhibited annually in Modern Art Associ-
ation exhibitions, Tokyo, 1960-1965; became a member of the
Association, 1962. Has worked in a public relations agency
since 1960. Lives in Hino City, Tokyo Prefecture. *One-man
shows:* Muramatsu Gallery, Tokyo, 1960; Akiyama Gallery,
Tokyo, 1962. In various group shows since 1959, including
"New Generation of Japanese Sculptors," National Museum
of Modern Art, Tokyo, 1963; "Contemporary Trend of Japanese
Paintings and Sculptures," National Museum of Modern Art,
Kyoto, 1964. Won prize from Modern Art Association, Tokyo.
1964, commissioned to do work by Seikei University, Tokyo.

104

Right, Mogami: *Laugh, Laugh, Laugh*. 1962. Pine, 66½ x 38 x
12". Lent by the artist.

Key Hiraga

Born in Tokyo, 1936. Studied economics at Keio University, Tokyo, 1954-1959. Since 1961, has worked in Editorial Department of *New Japan,* a pictorial annual published by Mainichi Newspaper. Has traveled in Italy, Spain and Switzerland; is presently spending a year in France. Lives in Tokyo. In group shows in Tokyo and Paris since 1956. Won third prize, Shell Award Exhibition, Tokyo, 1963; National New Artist Award, National Art Exhibition, Tokyo, 1964; International Young Artist Award, International Young Artists Exhibition, Tokyo, 1964.

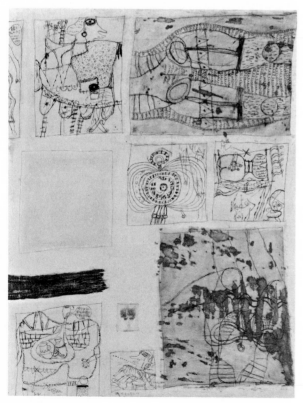

Hiraga: *The Window.* 1964. Oil on canvas, 57¼ x 44⅜".
Lent anonymously.

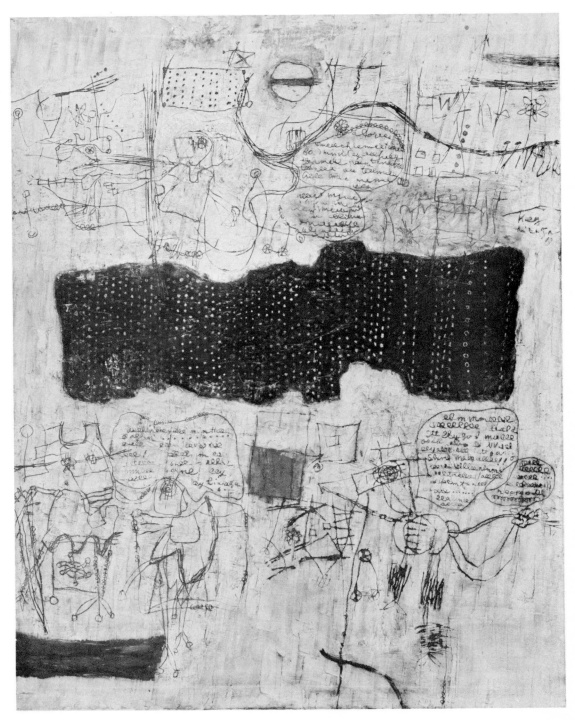

Hiraga: *A Day It Rained*. 1963. Oil on canvas, 63⅞ x 51¾". Yasuhiko Aoyagi, Tokyo.

Tomio Miki

Born in Tokyo, 1937. Graduated from Eisei School of Technology, Tokyo, 1957. Exhibited annually with Yomiuri Independents, Tokyo, 1958-1963. Lives in Tokyo. *One-man shows:* Kunugi Gallery, Tokyo, 1957, 1958, 1959; Bungei Shunju Gallery, Tokyo, 1961; Naika Gallery, Tokyo, 1963. In various group exhibitions in Japan since 1958, including "Young Seven," Minami Gallery, Tokyo, 1964; "Contemporary Trend of Japanese Art," National Museum of Modern Art, Tokyo, 1965. Won award, Contemporary Japanese Art Exhibition, Tokyo, 1964. Represented in collections of Louisiana Museum, Humlebaek, Denmark; Museum of Modern Art, New York.

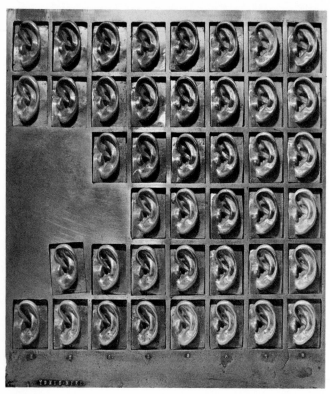

Right, Miki: *Untitled (Ear).* 1964. Cast aluminum, 34³/₈ x 21¹/₈ x 7¹/₂". The Charles R. Penney Collection, Olcott, New York.

Left, Miki: *Untitled (Ears).* 1964. Cast aluminum, 21³/₈ x 19 x 1¹/₂". The Museum of Modern Art, New York. Purchase.

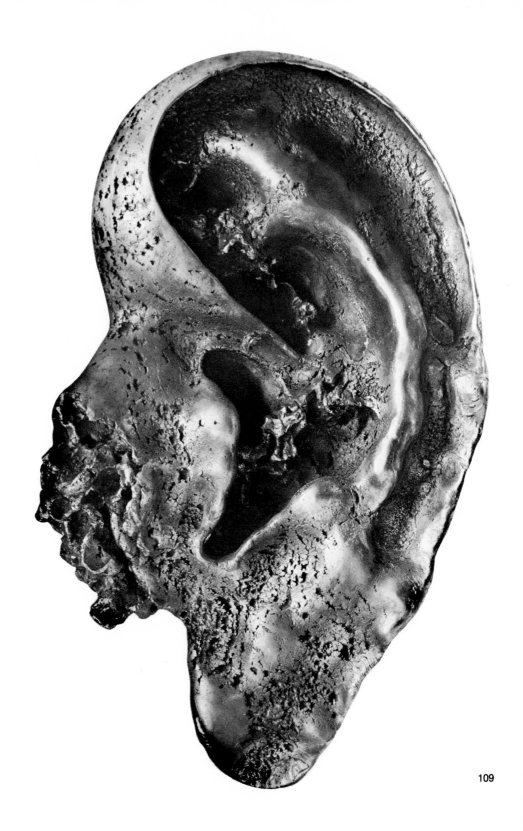

Shuji Mukai

Born in Kobe City, Hyogo Prefecture, 1939. Studied at Osaka
School of Art, 1958-1960. Became member of Gutai Art
Association, Osaka, 1959; has exhibited with them yearly since.
Lives in Kobe. *One-man show:* Gutai Pinacotheca, Osaka, 1963.
In various group exhibitions since 1959, including XII Premio
Lissone, Lissone (Italy), 1961; "Contemporary Trend of
Japanese Paintings and Sculptures," National Museum of
Modern Art, Kyoto, 1964; "First Exhibition for the Prize of the
Nagaoka Museum," Museum of Contemporary Art, Nagaoka,
1964. Represented in collections of Museum of Contemporary
Art, Nagaoka; Museum of Modern Art, New York; International
Center for Aesthetic Research, Turin.

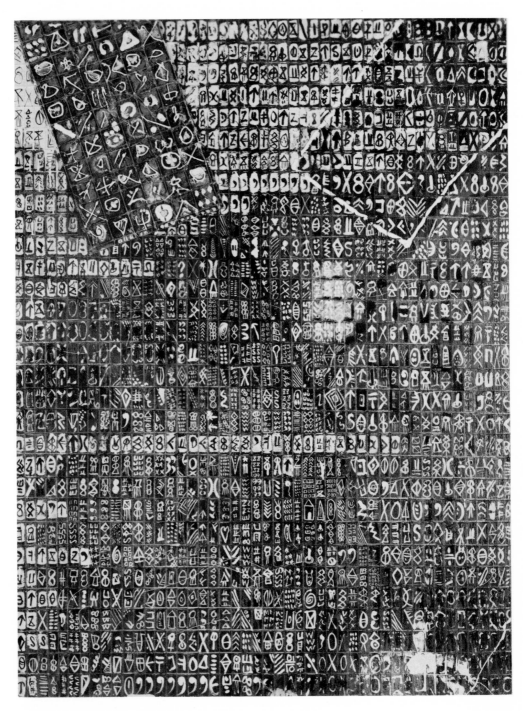

S. Mukai: *Untitled*. 1963. Oil on composition board, 72¹⁄₈ x 53⁷⁄₈". The Museum of Modern Art, New York. Purchase.

Keiji Usami

Born in Suita City, Osaka Prefecture, 1940. Graduated from Tennouji Senior High School, Osaka, 1958. Since 1959, has lived in Tokyo, where he teaches art privately. *One-man show:* Minami Gallery, Tokyo, 1963. In various group exhibitions, including "Contemporary Trend of Japanese Paintings and Sculptures," National Museum of Modern Art, Kyoto, 1964; "Moderne Malerei aus Japan," Kunsthaus, Zurich, 1965. Awarded First Stralem Prize, International Young Artists Exhibition, Tokyo, 1964.

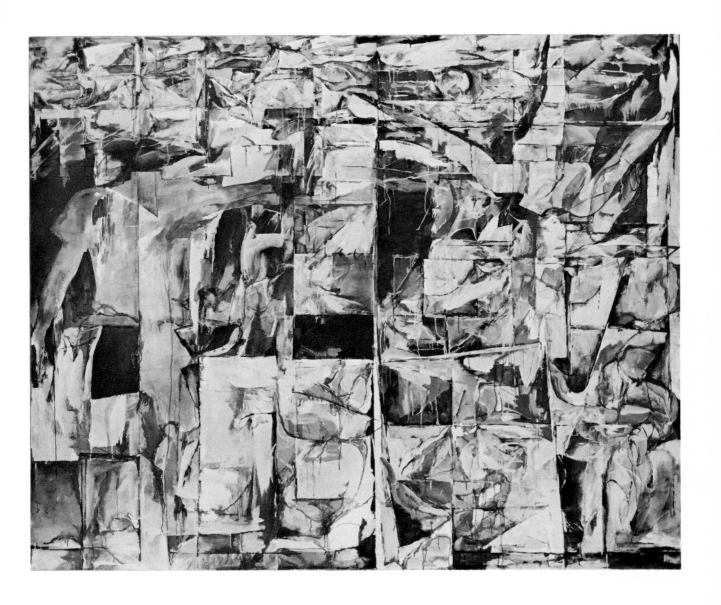

Usami: *The Milky Way Railroad*. 1964. Oil on canvas, 69¹/₈ x 88¹/₈″. Tetsusaburo Tanaka, Ichinomiya.

Lenders to the Exhibition

Nobuya Abe, Rome; Hiroshi Akana, Tokyo; Naotaro Akiyama, Tokyo; Yasuhiko Aoyagi, Tokyo; Mr. and Mrs. Robert M. Benjamin, New York; Mrs. Gilbert W. Chapman, New York; Mr. and Mrs. Hervey Parke Clark, Woodside, California; Hisao Domoto, Paris; Shyu Eguchi, Tokyo; Joseph H. Hirshhorn Collection, New York; Howard E. Johnson, Oakland, California; Takeshi Kawashima, New York; Reiji Kimura, New York; Nobuaki, Kojima, Tokyo; Mr. and Mrs. Samuel M. Kootz, New York; Shin Kuno, Nagoya; Masaaki Kusumoto, New York; Tomio Miki, Tokyo; Hisayuki Mogami, Tokyo; George Montgomery, New York; Sadamasa Motonaga, Takarazuka; Ryokichi Mukai, Tokyo; Shuji Mukai, Kobe; Natsuyuki Nakanishi, Tokyo; Minoru Niizuma, New York; Genmei Ohno, Tokyo; Shinjiro Okamoto, Tokyo; Mrs. Bliss Parkinson, New York; The Charles R. Penney Collection, Olcott, New York; Mr. and Mrs. John D. Rockefeller 3rd, New York; Mrs. Madeleine H. Russell, San Francisco; Mr. and Mrs. Robert W. Sarnoff, New York; Key Sato, Paris; Kusuo Shimizu, Tokyo; Morio Shinoda, Tokyo; Kazuo Shiraga, Amagasaki; Mrs. Emily B. Staempfli, New York; Mrs. Donald B. Straus, New York; Tetsusaburo Tanaka, Ichinomiya; Michel Tapié, Paris; Kakuzo Tatehata, Tokyo; Soichiro Tomioka, Tokyo; Mr. and Mrs. Burton Tremaine, New York; Mrs. Warren Tremaine, Santa Barbara, California; Shindo Tsuji, Kyoto; Waichi Tsutaka, Nishinomiya; Brooks Walker, San Francisco; Mrs. Robert F. Windfohr, Fort Worth, Texas; Kazuo Yagi, Kyoto; Katsuhiro Yamaguchi, Tokyo; Sei Yamamoto, Tokyo; Tokutaro Yamamura, Nishinomiya; Masanobu Yoshimura, New York.

Joslyn Art Museum, Omaha, Nebraska; The Museum of Contemporary Art, Nagaoka; The Museum of Modern Art, New York; San Francisco Museum of Art, San Francisco.

Galerie Suzanne De Coninck, Paris; Dwan Gallery, Los Angeles; Gutai Pinacotheca, Osaka; Kootz Gallery, New York; Galerie Jacques Massol, Paris; Minami Gallery, Tokyo; Betty Parsons Gallery, New York; Tokyo Gallery, Tokyo; Toninelli Arte Moderna, Milan; Willard Gallery, New York; Yamada Art Gallery, Kyoto.

Catalog of the Exhibition

An asterisk preceding the title indicates that the work is illustrated. In the dimensions, height precedes width.

Nobuya Abe

*_Gray Echo._ 1964. Encaustic and canvas on wood, $70\frac{1}{2}$ x $70\frac{1}{2}$". Mrs. John D. Rockefeller 3rd, New York. Ill. p. 41.

Hiroshi Akana

*_Pair._ 1963. Oil on canvas, $71\frac{3}{4}$ x $89\frac{1}{2}$". Lent by the artist. Ill. p. 55.

*_Fighting Spirit._ 1964. Oil on canvas, $71\frac{1}{2}$ x $89\frac{3}{4}$". Lent by the artist. Ill. p. 54.

Shusaku Arakawa

*_Card into Feather, Eternal Magic._ 1964. Oil on canvas, $63\frac{1}{4}$ x 91". Mrs. John D. Rockefeller 3rd, New York. Ill. p. 100.

Back and Front of Time: S. A. Equation. 1965. Oil on canvas, 89 x $63\frac{3}{4}$". Mrs. Bliss Parkinson, New York.

*_The Communicating Vases._ 1965. Oil on canvas with plastic assemblage, $89\frac{3}{8}$ x $63\frac{7}{8}$". Dwan Gallery, Los Angeles. Ill. p. 101.

Kengiro Azuma

*_MU S-56._ 1962. Bronze, $22\frac{1}{8}$" (including base) x $12\frac{1}{4}$". Toninelli Arte Moderna, Milan. Ill. p. 68.

*_MU S-116._ 1963. Bronze, $30\frac{5}{8}$ x $18\frac{1}{4}$ x $9\frac{1}{4}$". Toninelli Arte Moderna, Milan. Ill. p. 69.

Hisao Domoto

*_Solution of Continuity, 57._ 1963. 12-part screen, aluminum and canvas, each panel $63\frac{1}{8}$ x $15\frac{3}{4}$". Lent by the artist. Ill. p. 13.

*_Solution of Continuity, 22._ 1964. Oil on canvas, $38\frac{1}{8}$ x 51". Howard E. Johnson, Oakland, California. Ill. p. 74.

*_Solution of Continuity, 24._ 1964. Oil on canvas, $63\frac{5}{8}$ x $51\frac{1}{8}$". The Museum of Modern Art, New York. Gift of Mr. and Mrs. David Kluger. Ill. p. 75.

Shyu Eguchi

Vestige No. 7. 1963. Walnut, $20\frac{1}{2}$ x 9 x 8". Lent by Naotaro Akiyama, Tokyo.

*_Monument No. 1._ 1963. Cherry, $41\frac{3}{8}$ x 17 x $20\frac{3}{8}$". Mrs. Gilbert W. Chapman, New York. Ill. p. 82.

*_Monument No. 4._ 1964. Cherry, $18\frac{1}{4}$ x 22 x $14\frac{1}{4}$". The Museum of Modern Art, New York. Purchase. Ill. p. 83.

Key Hiraga

*_A Day It Rained._ 1963. Oil on canvas, $63\frac{7}{8}$ x $51\frac{3}{4}$". Yasuhiko Aoyagi, Tokyo. Ill. p. 107.

*_The Window._ 1964. Oil on canvas, $57\frac{1}{4}$ x $44\frac{3}{8}$". Lent anonymously. Ill. p. 106.

Genichiro Inokuma

*_Wall Street._ 1964. Oil on canvas, $80\frac{1}{8}$ x $70\frac{1}{8}$". San Francisco Museum of Art. Gift of Mrs. Madeleine Haas Russell. Ill. pp. 16, 25.

Yukihisa Isobe

*_Untitled._ 1964. Assemblage, $71\frac{3}{4}$ x $71\frac{1}{2}$ x $2\frac{1}{2}$". Brooks Walker, San Francisco. Ill. p. 103.

Shigeru Izumi

*_Painting._ 1964. Oil on canvas, 35 x $45\frac{3}{4}$". Mrs. John D. Rockefeller 3rd, New York. Ill. p. 56.

*_Painting._ 1965. Oil on canvas, $44\frac{7}{8}$ x $57\frac{1}{2}$". Galerie Suzanne De Coninck, Paris. Ill. p. 57.

Minoru Kawabata

*_Dark Oval._ 1964. Oil on canvas, $63\frac{7}{8}$ x $51\frac{3}{8}$". Mrs. John D. Rockefeller 3rd, New York. Ill. pp. 20, 36.

*_March._ 1964. Oil on canvas, $63\frac{3}{4}$ x $51\frac{3}{8}$". Betty Parsons Gallery, New York. Ill. p. 37.

Takeshi Kawashima

*_Untitled 1964, New York._ Center panel of a triptych. 1964. Oil on canvas, $100\frac{1}{2}$ x 80". The Museum of Modern Art, New York. Purchase. Ill. pp. 20, 77.

Mokuma Kikuhata

*_Roulette: Ancient Shield._ 1964. Enamel paint and assemblage

on wood, 38³/₈ x 31¹/₈ x 4³/₄″. Mrs. John D. Rockefeller 3rd, New York. Ill. p. 95.
*Roulette: Number Five. 1964. Enamel paint and assemblage on wood, 42¹/₈ x 25¹/₂ x 8¹/₂″. The Museum of Modern Art, New York. Purchase. Ill. p. 18.
*Roulette: Target. 1964. Enamel paint and assemblage on wood, 48 x 33¹/₄ x 6¹/₈″. Lent anonymously. Ill. p. 94.

Reiji Kimura
*No. 164. 1964. Oil and metal paint on paper and canvas, 72⁵/₈ x 52¹/₂″. Lent by the artist. Ill. p. 71.
*No. S. A. 1964. Oil and metal paint on paper and composition board, 15¹/₂ x 14³/₈″. George Montgomery, New York. Ill. p. 70.

Nobuaki Kojima
*Untitled (Figure). 1964. Painted plaster, cloth and polyester 69 x 44¹/₂ x 20³/₄″. Lent by the artist. Ill. p. 97.
*Untitled (Figure). 1964. Painted plaster, cloth and polyester, 68⁵/₈ x 43³/₄ x 18¹/₄″. Lent by the artist. Ill. pp. 19, 97.
*Untitled (Figure). 1964. Painted plaster, cloth and polyester, 67³/₄ x 37¹/₄ x 20¹/₂″. Lent anonymously. Ill. p. 97.
Untitled (Two Flags, Red and Blue). 1964. Cloth and polyester. Red flag: 51¹/₂ x 38¹/₂ x 2¹/₂″. Blue flag: 64 x 11 x 7¹/₄″. Lent by the artist.

Shin Kuno
*Untitled. 1961. Lacquered steel relief mounted on wood, 50¹/₈ x 35⁷/₈ x 2¹/₈″. Lent anonymously. Ill. p. 53.
*Untitled. 1963. Lacquered steel relief mounted on wood, 50¹/₈ x 35⁷/₈ x 1³/₄″. Mrs. John D. Rockefeller 3rd, New York. Ill. p. 52.
Untitled. 1963. Lacquered steel relief mounted on wood, 63 x 51¹/₈ x 2¹/₄″. The Museum of Contemporary Art, Nagaoka.

Masaaki Kusumoto
*Environment and Movement. 1964. Synthetic polymer paint and metal foil on canvas, 110¹/₄ x 120¹/₈″. Lent by the artist. Ill. p. 89.

Tomio Miki
*Untitled (Ear). 1964. Cast aluminum, 34³/₈ x 21¹/₈ x 7¹/₂″. The Charles R. Penney Collection, Olcott, New York. Ill. p. 109.
*Untitled (Ears). 1964. Cast aluminum, 21³/₈ x 19 x 1¹/₂″. The Museum of Modern Art, New York. Purchase. Ill. p. 108.
Untitled. 1964. Oil on plexiglas, 52³/₄ x 43¹/₂ x 9″. Minami Gallery, Tokyo.

Hisayuki Mogami
*Laugh, Laugh, Laugh. 1962. Pine, 66¹/₂ x 38 x 12″. Lent by the artist. Ill. p. 105.

Sadamasa Motonaga
*Untitled. 1963. Oil and gravel on canvas, 72¹/₈ x 50¹/₄″. Tokyo Gallery, Tokyo. Ill. p. 14.
*Untitled. 1964. Oil on canvas, 36¹/₈ x 45⁵/₈″. Lent anonymously. Ill. p. 60.
*Untitled. 1964. Oil on canvas, 108¹/₄ x 70¹/₄″. Lent by the artist. Ill. p. 61.

Ryokichi Mukai
*The Ants' Castle. 1960. Cast and welded metal alloy, 32⁷/₈″

(including base) x 29⁵/₈ x 11¹/₂″. Lent by the artist. Ill. p. 46.
*The Horse Fly. 1962. Cast and welded aluminum, 32¹/₂ x 21¹/₄ x 18¹/₂″. Mrs. John D. Rockefeller 3rd, New York. Ill. p. 47.

Shuji Mukai
*Untitled. 1963. Oil on composition board, 72¹/₈ x 53⁷/₈″. The Museum of Modern Art, New York. Purchase. Ill. p. 111.
Untitled. 1964. Oil on canvas, 72 x 108″. Mr. and Mrs. Hervey Parke Clark, Woodside, California.
Untitled. 1964. Oil on canvas, 72¹/₄ x 72³/₈″. The Museum of Contemporary Art, Nagaoka.

Masayuki Nagare
*Plowing. 1958. Granite, 14¹/₄ x 12¹/₄ x 10³/₈″. Mr. and Mrs. Robert M. Benjamin, New York. Ill. p. 62.
*Enclosure. 1959. Granite, 8¹/₂ x 22³/₄ x 17″. Mrs. John D. Rockefeller 3rd, New York. Ill. p. 63.
Court Figure. 1959-60. Granite, 15³/₄ x 18¹/₄ x 14″. Mrs. John D. Rockefeller 3rd, New York.
*Windwoven. 1962. Granite, 11¹/₄ x 28³/₈ x 19¹/₄″. Mrs. Emily B. Staempfli, New York. Ill. p. 62.

Natsuyuki Nakanishi
Compact Objects (4). 1961. Plaster, sand and lacquer, each 9¹/₂ x 6 x 6″. Lent anonymously.
*Compact Objects (6). 1962. Assemblages contained in polyester, each 9 x 5⁷/₈ x 5⁷/₈″. Lent by the artist; Mrs. John D. Rockefeller 3rd, New York; Mrs. Warren Tremaine, Santa Barbara, California; and The Museum of Modern Art, New York (Purchase). Ill. pp. 18, 99.

Minoru Niizuma
*The Waves' Voice. 1963. Granite, 27⁷/₈ x 20¹/₂ x 5″. Mrs. John D. Rockefeller 3rd, New York. Ill. p. 79.
*Castle of the Eye. 1964. Marble, 18¹/₂ x 15³/₄ x 8″. The Museum of Modern Art, New York. Purchase. Ill. p. 78.

Shinjiro Okamoto
*The Big Laugh. 1963. Acrylic on canvas, 63⁷/₈ x 44¹/₄″. Mrs. Robert F. Windfohr, Fort Worth, Texas. Ill. p. 91.
*Ninth Little Indian. 1964. Acrylic on canvas, 57¹/₂ x 38¹/₄″. Mrs. Robert F. Windfohr, Fort Worth, Texas. Ill. p. 90.
*A Western Dog. 1964. Acrylic on canvas, 35¹/₄ x 51¹/₄″. Minami Gallery, Tokyo. Ill. p. 18.

Toshinobu Onosato
*Untitled. 1961. Oil on canvas, 24 x 28³/₄″. Genmei Ohno, Tokyo. Ill. p. 39.
*Untitled. 1962. Oil on canvas, 28⁷/₈ x 36″. Mr. and Mrs. John D. Rockefeller 3rd, New York. Ill. p. 16.
Untitled. 1964. Oil on canvas, 24 x 28⁷/₈″. Minami Gallery, Tokyo.
*Untitled. 1964. Oil on canvas, 24 x 28³/₄″. Mrs. John D. Rockefeller 3rd, New York. Ill. p. 38.

Yoshishige Saito
Untitled (red). 1960. Oil on wood, 71⁵/₈ x 48″. Tokutaro Yamamura, Nishinomiya.
Untitled (blue). 1960. Oil on wood, 72 x 48″. Tokutaro Yamamura, Nishinomiya.

Untitled (red). 1962. Oil on wood, 71³/₄ x 47³/₄". Mrs. John D. Rockefeller 3rd, New York. Ill. pp. 15, 26.

Untitled (blue). 1962. Oil on wood, 71⁵/₈ x 47³/₄". Howard E. Johnson, Oakland, California. Ill. p. 27.

Key Sato

Wall Myth. 1960-62. Oil on canvas, 79 x 59¹/₈". Galerie Jacques Massol, Paris.

Of the Essence. 1960-63. Oil on burlap, 36¹/₈ x 28⁵/₈". Lent by the artist. Ill. p. 30.

History of Space (black). 1965. Oil on canvas, 63⁷/₈ x 51¹/₄". Mrs. John D. Rockefeller 3rd, New York. Ill. p. 31.

Morio Shinoda

Tension and Compression. 1960. Bronze and wire, 19 x 15³/₈ x 7¹/₄". Lent anonymously. Ill. p. 80.

Tension and Compression. 1962. Bronze and wire, 26⁷/₈ x 33 x 23⁷/₈". Mrs. John D. Rockefeller 3rd, New York. Ill. p. 81.

Kazuo Shiraga

Untitled. 1964. Oil on canvas, 85¹/₂ x 95⁵/₈". The Museum of Contemporary Art, Nagaoka. Ill. p. 65.

Untitled. 1964. Oil on canvas, 51¹/₂ x 76³/₈". Lent anonymously. Ill. p. 64.

Kumi Sugaï

Oni. 1956. Oil on canvas, 78³/₄ x 61³/₄". Mr. and Mrs. Samuel M. Kootz, New York. Ill. p. 51.

Tadasky (Tadasuke Kuwayama)

T-104. 1965. Acrylic on canvas, 68 x 68". Kootz Gallery, New York. Ill. p. 93.

Atsuko Tanaka

Untitled. 1964. Vinyl on canvas, 77¹/₄ x 52". Minami Gallery, Tokyo. Ill. p. 87.

Untitled. 1964. Vinyl on canvas, 131³/₈ x 88⁷/₈". The Museum of Modern Art, New York. Purchase. Ill. p. 17.

Kakuzo Tatehata

Gate. 1964. Cast cement, 69¹/₈ x 46 x 13". Mrs. Madeleine H. Russell, San Francisco. Ill. p. 49.

Soichiro Tomioka

Untitled. April, 1964. Oil on canvas, 63⁷/₈ x 63³/₄". Mrs. John D. Rockefeller 3rd, New York.

Untitled. May, 1964. Oil on canvas, 63⁷/₈ x 63³/₄". Mrs. Bliss Parkinson, New York. Ill. p. 59.

Untitled. August, 1964. Oil on canvas, 64 x 63³/₄". Lent by the artist. Ill. p. 58.

Tomonori Toyofuku

Adrift, III. 1960. Wood, 83⁷/₈ x 120 x 33". The Museum of Modern Art, New York. Philip C. Johnson Fund. Ill. p. 67.

Sui, III. 1964. Bronze, 80¹/₈ x 19 x 9⁷/₈". Joseph H. Hirshhorn Collection, New York. Ill. p. 66.

Ventus. 1964. Wood, 55³/₈ x 45¹/₄". Mr. and Mrs. Robert W. Sarnoff, New York. Ill. p. 67.

Shindo Tsuji

Jomon. 1959. Terra-cotta, 45¹/₄ x 17⁵/₈ x 7¹/₂". Yamada Art Gallery, Kyoto. Ill. p. 32.

Han Shan. 1961. Terra-cotta, 39 x 24³/₄ x 9". Mr. and Mrs. John D. Rockefeller 3rd, New York. Ill. p. 33.

Waichi Tsutaka

Black and White. 1961. Oil on canvas, 38¹/₄ x 57¹/₄". Mrs. John D. Rockefeller 3rd, New York.

Cosmos. 1963. Oil on canvas, 35³/₄ x 25⁷/₈". Lent by the artist. Ill. p. 34.

Accept the Inevitable. 1964. Oil on canvas, 51¹/₄ x 76". Mrs. Donald B. Straus, New York. Ill. p. 35.

Untitled. 1964. Oil on canvas, 46 x 31³/₄". Joslyn Art Museum, Omaha, Nebraska. Ill. p. 15.

Keiji Usami

Untitled. 1963. Oil on canvas, 72³/₄ x 94¹/₂". Minami Gallery, Tokyo.

The Milky Way Railroad. 1964. Oil on canvas, 69¹/₈ x 88¹/₈". Tetsusaburo Tanaka, Ichinomiya. Ill. p. 113.

Kazuo Yagi

A Cloud Remembered. 1962. Ceramic, 16" (including base) x 9³/₄ x 8¹/₄". The Museum of Modern Art, New York. Purchase. Ill. p. 45.

Queen. 1964. Black ceramic, 12³/₄" (including base) x 10¹/₈ x 9⁷/₈". San Francisco Museum of Art. Gift of Mrs. Ferdinand C. Smith. Ill. p. 44.

Saint. 1964. Black ceramic, 4 x 9⁷/₈ x 9⁷/₈". Mrs. John D. Rockefeller 3rd, New York.

Untitled. 1964. Black ceramic, 9⁵/₈ x 10¹/₂ x 9³/₄". Lent anonymously.

Katsuhiro Yamaguchi

Jet. 1964. Cloth stretched over metal wire, 65 x 79 x 42¹/₂". Lent by the artist. Ill. p. 73.

Takeo Yamaguchi

Enshin. 1961. Oil on wood, 71⁷/₈ x 71⁷/₈". Minami Gallery, Tokyo. Ill. p. 23.

Sei Yamamoto

Sarusawa Pond. 1964. Oil on canvas, 63⁷/₈ x 51¹/₂". Mrs. John D. Rockefeller 3rd, New York. Ill. p. 42.

Yoshino Path. 1964. Oil on canvas, 51³/₈ x 63³/₄". Mr. and Mrs. John D. Rockefeller 3rd, New York. Ill. p. 43.

Jiro Yoshihara

Untitled. 1962. Oil on canvas, 71⁵/₈ x 107¹/₄". Michel Tapié, Paris. Ill. p. 29.

Masanobu Yoshimura

Coffer. 1963. Plaster on wood, with canvas interior, 32 x 25¹/₂ x 17¹/₂". Lent by the artist. Ill. p. 84.

Two Columns. 1964. Plaster on wood, with base and plexiglas vitrine. 74¹/₄" (including base) x 36 x 17⁷/₈". The Museum of Modern Art, New York. Purchase. Ill. p. 85.